W9-AOS-583

Made from scratch

PASTA

EVERYDAY EASY HOME COOKING

This edition published by Parragon Books Ltd in 2014 and distributed by

Parragon Inc.
440 Park Avenue South, 13th Floor
New York, NY 10016
www.parragon.com/lovefood

LOVE FOOD is an imprint of Parragon Books Ltd

Copyright © Parragon Books Ltd 2012–2014

LOVE FOOD and the accompanying heart device is a registered trademark of
Parragon Books Ltd in the USA, the UK, Australia, India, and the EU.

All rights reserved. No part of this publication may be reproduced, stored
in a retrieval system, or transmitted, in any form or by any means, electric,
mechanical, photocopying, recording, or otherwise, without the prior permission
of the copyright holder.

ISBN 978-1-4723-2997-4

Printed in China

Cover photography by Ian Garlick
New photography by Clive Bozzard-Hill
New home economy by Valerie Barrett, Carol Tennant,
Sally Mansfield and Mitzie Wilson
New recipes and introduction by Linda Doeser
Edited by Fiona Biggs
Nutritional analysis by Fiona Hunter

Notes for the Reader
This book uses standard kitchen measuring spoons and cups. All spoon and cup
measurements are level unless otherwise indicated. Unless otherwise stated,
milk is assumed to be whole, eggs are large, individual vegetables are medium,
and pepper is freshly ground black pepper. Unless otherwise stated, all root
vegetables should be peeled prior to using.

Garnishes, decorations, and serving suggestions are all optional and not
necessarily included in the recipe ingredients or method. Any optional
ingredients and seasoning to taste are not included in the nutritional analysis.
The times given are only an approximate guide. Preparation times differ
according to the techniques used by different people and the cooking times
may also vary from those given. Optional ingredients, variations, or serving
suggestions have not been included in the time calculations.

Vegetarians should be aware that some of the prepared ingredients used in the
recipes in this book may contain animal products. Always check the package
before use.

Contents

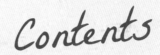

Introduction 4

Vegetarian 6

Meat & Poultry 36

Fish & Seafood 66

Sauces 96

Index 126

Introduction

Pasta's immense popularity is hardly surprising, given that it is astonishingly versatile, easy to cook, nourishing, inexpensive and, in its dried form, keeps for ages. In short, it is arguably the most useful ingredient in the kitchen.

It goes with just about every other foodstuff imaginable to create a range of taste sensations—rich and creamy, light and refreshing, hot and spicy, simple and basic, or luxurious and impressive. It may be served hot as a main course or cold as a substantial salad or as part of a picnic, buffet, or barbecue and is a delicious and valuable addition to all kinds of soups. It is as tasty partnered with vegetarian ingredients, from tomatoes and mushrooms, to cheese and herbs, as it is with all kinds of meat and poultry, fish and seafood.

Pasta is the perfect choice for today's busy lifestyle as there are many dishes that can be prepared and cooked within 30 minutes and some that take only half that time. It's great for midweek family meals, especially as almost all children really love it, and is also ideal for easy, informal entertaining. Whether you're looking for a warming and filling supper to serve on a chilly winter's evening or a delicately flavored alfresco summer lunch, pasta fits the bill.

Nutritionists recommend that cereals should comprise 33 per cent of a well-balanced diet. Pasta is high in complex carbohydrates, providing a steady release of energy, as well as being an important source of fiber. It contains very little fat. Depending on the type of pasta, it can be a useful source of protein as well as important minerals and vitamins.

Pasta needs a lot of room and a lot of water to cook perfectly, so use a large saucepan.

Pasta is very versatile so it's easy to find fabulous recipes for all occasions and every season of the year.

Macaroni & Double Cheese *8*

Tomato, Olive & Mozzarella Pasta Salad *10*

Spinach & Ricotta Cannelloni *12*

Fresh Tomato Soup with Pasta *14*

Penne with Asparagus & Blue Cheese *16*

Pumpkin Ravioli *18*

Chile Broccoli Pasta *20*

Spaghetti Olio E Aglio *22*

Ziti with Arugula *24*

Spicy Vegetable Lasagna *26*

Pasta with Leek & Butternut Squash *28*

Mushroom Cannelloni *30*

Hearty Bean & Pasta Soup *32*

Pappardelle with Cherry Tomatoes, Arugula & Mozzarella *34*

Vegetarian

Macaroni & Double Cheese

 SERVES 4

PREP TIME:
10 minutes

COOKING TIME:
15 minutes

nutritional information
per serving — 1,109 cal, 66g fat, 24g sat fat, 9g total sugars, 3g salt

This is an especially rich and tasty variation of a family favorite, equally popular with children and adults.

INGREDIENTS

8 ounces dried macaroni

1 cup vegetarian ricotta cheese

1½ tablespoons whole-grain mustard

3 tablespoons snipped fresh chives, plus extra to garnish

12 cherry tomatoes, halved

⅔ cup drained and chopped sun-dried tomatoes in oil

butter or oil, for greasing

1 cup shredded vegetarian cheddar cheese

salt and pepper

1. Preheat the broiler to high. Bring a large saucepan of lightly salted water to a boil. Add the pasta, bring back to a boil, and cook for 8–10 minutes, or according to the package directions, until tender but still firm to the bite. Drain.

2. In a large bowl, mix the vegetarian ricotta cheese with the mustard and chives and season with salt and pepper.

3. Stir in the macaroni, cherry tomatoes, and sun-dried tomatoes and mix well.

4. Grease a 2-quart shallow ovenproof dish. Spoon in the macaroni mixture, spreading evenly.

5. Sprinkle the vegetarian cheddar cheese over the macaroni mixture and cook under the preheated broiler for 4–5 minutes, until golden and bubbling. Serve the macaroni immediately, sprinkled with extra chives.

2

3

5

COOK'S NOTE

For an even richer dish, tear 4 ounces vegetarian mozzarella cheese into small pieces and stir into the macaroni with the tomatoes.

Tomato, Olive & Mozzarella Pasta Salad

 SERVES 4   PREP TIME: 5 minutes   COOKING TIME: 10 minutes

nutritional information per serving	385 cal, 36g fat, 10g sat fat, 8g total sugars, 0.7g salt

When you taste this classic combination of ingredients, you'll know why it is so popular in Italy.

INGREDIENTS

8 ounces dried conchiglie (pasta shells)

⅓ cup pine nuts

2½ cups halved cherry tomatoes

1 red bell pepper, seeded and cut into bite-size chunks

1 red onion, chopped

8 ounces vegetarian mozzarella cheese, cut into small pieces

12 ripe black olives, pitted

1 cup fresh basil leaves

vegetarian Parmesan-style cheese shavings, to garnish

salt

dressing

⅓ cup extra virgin olive oil

2 tablespoons balsamic vinegar

1 tablespoon chopped fresh basil

salt and pepper

1. Bring a large saucepan of lightly salted water to a boil. Add the pasta, bring back to a boil, and cook for 8–10 minutes, or according to the package directions, until tender but still firm to the bite. Drain thoroughly and let cool.

2. Meanwhile, heat a dry skillet over low heat, add the pine nuts, and cook, shaking the skillet frequently, for 1–2 minutes, until lightly toasted. Remove from the heat, transfer to a dish, and let cool.

3. To make the dressing, put all the ingredients in a small bowl and mix together well. Cover with plastic wrap and set aside.

4. Divide the pasta among four serving bowls. Add the pine nuts, tomatoes, bell pepper, onion, vegetarian mozzarella cheese, and olives to each bowl. Sprinkle with the basil, then drizzle with the dressing. Garnish with vegetarian Parmesan-style cheese shavings and serve.

Spinach & Ricotta Cannelloni

 SERVES 4

PREP TIME:
20 minutes

COOKING TIME:
40–45 minutes

nutritional information per serving	591 cal, 28g fat, 16g sat fat, 9g total sugars, 1.1g salt

Cannelloni started life as sheets of pasta—lasagna noodles—which were rolled around a filling, but now tubes of pasta, ready for stuffing, are available.

INGREDIENTS

melted butter, for greasing

12 dried cannelloni tubes, each about 3 inches long

salt and pepper

filling

½ (10-ounce) package frozen spinach, thawed and drained

½ cup vegetarian ricotta cheese

1 egg

3 tablespoons grated vegetarian pecorino cheese

pinch of freshly grated nutmeg

cheese sauce

2 tablespoons butter

2 tablespoons all-purpose flour

2½ cups hot whole milk

¾ cup shredded vegetarian Gruyère cheese

1. Preheat the oven to 350°F. Grease a rectangular ovenproof dish with the melted butter.

2. Bring a large saucepan of lightly salted water to a boil. Add the pasta, bring back to a boil, and cook for 6–7 minutes, or according to the package directions, until nearly tender. Drain and rinse, then spread out on a clean dish towel.

3. To make the filling, put the spinach and vegetarian ricotta cheese into a food processor or blender and process briefly until combined. Add the egg and vegetarian pecorino cheese and process to a smooth paste. Transfer to a bowl, add the nutmeg, and season with salt and pepper.

4. Spoon the filling into a pastry bag fitted with a ½-inch tip. Carefully open a cannelloni tube and pipe in a little of the filling. Place the filled tube in the prepared dish and repeat.

5. To make the cheese sauce, melt the butter in a saucepan. Add the flour to the butter and cook over low heat, stirring continuously, for 1 minute. Remove from the heat and gradually stir in the hot milk. Return to the heat and bring to a boil, stirring continuously. Simmer over low heat, stirring frequently, for 10 minutes, until thickened and smooth.

6. Remove from the heat, stir in the vegetarian Gruyère cheese, and season with salt and pepper.

7. Spoon the cheese sauce over the filled cannelloni. Cover the dish with aluminum foil and bake in the preheated oven for 20–25 minutes. Serve immediately.

Fresh Tomato Soup
with Pasta

 SERVES 4　　PREP TIME: 15 minutes　　COOKING TIME: 1 hour

nutritional information per serving	135 cal, 3.5g fat, 0.6g sat fat, 6g total sugars, 0.4g salt

Tomatoes are our major source of dietary lycopene, a carotene antioxidant that fights heart disease and may help prevent prostate cancer. They also contain vitamin C, quercetin, and lutein.

INGREDIENTS

1 tablespoon olive oil
4 large plum tomatoes
1 onion, cut into quarters
1 garlic clove, thinly sliced
1 celery stalk, coarsely chopped
2 cups vegetable stock
2 ounces dried soup pasta
salt and pepper
chopped fresh flat-leaf parsley, to garnish

1. Pour the oil into a large, heavy saucepan and add the tomatoes, onion, garlic, and celery. Cover and cook over low heat, occasionally shaking gently, for 45 minutes, until pulpy.

2. Transfer the mixture to a food processor or blender and process to a smooth puree.

3. Push the puree through a strainer into a clean saucepan.

4. Add the stock and bring to a boil. Add the pasta, bring back to a boil, and cook for 8–10 minutes, or according to the package directions, until the pasta is tender but still firm to the bite. Season with salt and pepper. Ladle into warm bowls, garnish with parsley, and serve immediately.

1

3

4

VARIATION:
Replace the chopped
fresh parsley with
chopped fresh chives
and serve with freshly
grated vegetarian
Parmesan-style cheese
sprinkled on the top.

Penne with Asparagus & Blue Cheese

 SERVES 4

PREP TIME:
10 minutes

COOKING TIME:
25 minutes

nutritional information
per serving

805 cal, 48g fat, 28g sat fat, 5g total sugars, 1.1g salt

It's hard to believe that a dish so stunning is also so simple and requires almost no effort to prepare.

INGREDIENTS

1 pound asparagus spears
1 tablespoon olive oil
8 ounces vegetarian
blue cheese, crumbled
¾ cup heavy cream
12 ounces dried penne
salt and pepper

1. Preheat the oven to 450°F. Place the asparagus spears in a single layer in a shallow ovenproof dish. Sprinkle with the oil and season with salt and pepper. Turn to coat in the oil and seasoning. Roast in the preheated oven for 10–12 minutes, until slightly browned and just tender. Set aside and keep warm.

2. Combine the cheese with the cream in a bowl. Season with salt and pepper.

3. Bring a large saucepan of lightly salted water to a boil. Add the pasta, bring back to a boil, and cook for 8–10 minutes, or according to the package directions, until tender but still firm to the bite. Drain and transfer to a warm serving dish. Immediately add the asparagus and the cheese mixture. Toss well until the cheese has melted and the pasta is coated with the sauce. Serve immediately.

1

2

3

GOES WELL WITH
Freshly baked sourdough
bread would be just the
thing for mopping up
every last bit of this
delicious creamy sauce.

Pumpkin Ravioli

 SERVES 4

PREP TIME:
30 minutes
plus chilling

COOKING TIME:
30-35 minutes

nutritional information
per serving   452 cal, 16g fat, 5g sat fat, 3g total sugars, 0.9g salt

This fabulous filled pasta is a favorite in Emilia-Romagna, a region of northern Italy that is famous for its pasta.

INGREDIENTS

1 ½ cups semolina flour, plus extra for dusting

2 eggs, beaten

1 tablespoon oil

½ teaspoon salt

1 teaspoon vinegar

3–4 tablespoons water

filling

1 tablespoon olive oil

4 cups pumpkin or butternut squash cubes

1 shallot, finely diced

½ cup water, plus extra for brushing

⅔ cup grated vegetarian Parmesan-stye cheese

1 egg, beaten

1 tablespoon finely chopped fresh parsley

salt and pepper

1. Knead the flour, eggs, oil, salt, vinegar, and water into a silky smooth dough. Wrap the dough in plastic wrap and chill in the refrigerator for 1 hour.

2. To make the filling, heat the olive oil in a saucepan, add the pumpkin and shallot, and sauté for 2-3 minutes, or until the shallot is translucent. Add the water and cook the pumpkin for 15-20 minutes, or until the liquid evaporates. Cool slightly, then mix with the cheese, egg, and parsley. Season with salt and pepper.

3. Divide the dough in half. Thinly roll out both pieces. Place small spoonfuls of the pumpkin mixture about 1 ½ inches apart on one sheet of dough. Brush a little water on the spaces in between. Lay the second sheet of dough on top and press down around each piece of filling.

4. Use a pastry wheel to cut out squares and press the edges together with a fork. Let the ravioli dry for 30 minutes, then bring a large saucepan of lightly salted water to a boil. Add the ravioli, bring back to a boil and cook over medium heat for 5-7 minutes, until tender, but still firm to the bite. Remove the ravioli with a slotted spoon and drain well on paper towels. Serve immediately.

Chile Broccoli Pasta

 SERVES 4   PREP TIME: 5 minutes   COOKING TIME: 10–15 minutes

nutritional information per serving	300 cal, 11g fat, 1.5g sat fat, 3g total sugars, trace salt

A dish made with these ingredients can't fail—they just seem right together. Good for serving to a crowd.

INGREDIENTS

8 ounces dried penne or macaroni

3 cups broccoli florets

¼ cup extra virgin olive oil

2 large garlic cloves, chopped

2 fresh red chiles, seeded and diced

8 cherry tomatoes

handful of fresh basil leaves, to garnish

salt

1. Bring a large saucepan of lightly salted water to a boil. Add the pasta, return to a boil, and cook for 8-10 minutes, or according to the package directions, until tender but still firm to the bite. Drain the pasta, refresh under cold running water, and drain again. Set aside.

2. Bring a separate saucepan of lightly salted water to a boil, add the broccoli, and cook for 5 minutes. Drain, refresh under cold running water, and drain again.

3. Heat the oil in a large, heavy skillet over high heat. Add the garlic, chiles, and tomatoes and cook, stirring continuously, for 1 minute.

4. Add the broccoli and mix well. Cook for 2 minutes, stirring, to heat all the way through. Add the pasta and mix well again. Cook for an additional minute. Transfer the pasta to a large, warm serving bowl and serve immediately, garnished with basil leaves.

2

3

4

COOK'S NOTE
Don't be tempted
to chop fresh
basil with a
knife—it will turn
black. Use small
leaves or tear
larger ones
into pieces.

Spaghetti Olio E Aglio

 SERVES 4   PREP TIME: 5 minutes   COOKING TIME: 10 minutes

nutritional information per serving	590 cal, 25g fat, 3.5g sat fat, 3.5g total sugars, trace salt

An inexpensive dish created by the poor, this classic from Rome is now popular throughout Italy.

INGREDIENTS

1 pound dried spaghetti
½ cup extra virgin olive oil
3 garlic cloves, finely chopped
3 tablespoons chopped fresh flat-leaf parsley
salt and pepper

1. Bring a large saucepan of lightly salted water to a boil. Add the pasta, bring back to a boil, and cook for 8–10 minutes, or according to the package directions, until tender but still firm to the bite.

2. Meanwhile, heat the oil in a heavy skillet. Add the garlic and a pinch of salt and cook over low heat, stirring continuously, for 3–4 minutes, or until golden. Do not let the garlic brown or it will taste bitter. Remove the skillet from the heat.

3. Drain the pasta and transfer to a warm serving dish. Pour in the garlic-flavored oil, then add the chopped parsley and season with salt and pepper. Toss well and serve immediately.

TO SERVE
Cooked pasta gets
cold quickly, so make
sure to transfer to a
warm serving plate
once drained.

Ziti with Arugula

|O| SERVES 4   PREP TIME: 20 minutes plus resting   COOKING TIME: 20 minutes

nutritional information per serving	435 cal, 16g fat, 2g sat fat, 2.5g total sugars, trace salt

This pungent dish from Puglia in the "heel" of Italy looks and tastes absolutely delicious.

INGREDIENTS

2 fresh red chiles, thinly sliced, plus 4 whole chiles to garnish

12 ounces dried ziti, broken into 1½-inch lengths

⅓ cup extra virgin olive oil

2 garlic cloves, left whole

1½ (5-ounce) packages arugula

grated vegetarian Parmesan-style cheese, to serve

1. For the red chile garnish, use a sharp knife to remove the tip and cut the chile lengthwise, almost to the stem. Seed and repeat the cutting process to create "petals" of an equal length. Place the flowers in a bowl of iced water for 15-20 minutes to encourage the petals to fan out.

2. Bring a large saucepan of lightly salted water to a boil. Add the pasta, bring back to a boil, and cook for 8–10 minutes, or according to the package directions, until tender but still firm to the bite.

3. Meanwhile, heat the oil in a large, heavy skillet. Add the garlic, arugula, and sliced chiles and sauté for 5 minutes, or until the arugula has wilted.

4. Stir 2 tablespoons of the pasta cooking water into the arugula, then drain the pasta and add to the skillet. Cook, stirring frequently, for 2 minutes, then transfer to a warm serving dish. Remove and discard the garlic cloves and chiles, garnish with the red chile flowers, and serve immediately with the Parmesan-style cheese.

1

3

4

GOES WELL WITH
This would be good
with plum tomatoes
roasted with garlic,
dressed with olive oil
and balsamic vinegar
and served warm
or cold.

Spicy Vegetable Lasagna

 SERVES 4 | PREP TIME: 15 minutes plus standing time | COOKING TIME: 55 minutes

nutritional information per serving	534 cal, 28g fat, 12g sat fat, 15g total sugars, 0.8g salt

This colorful and tasty lasagna has layers of diced and sliced vegetables in tomato sauce, all topped with a rich cheese sauce.

INGREDIENTS

1 eggplant, sliced
3 tablespoons olive oil
2 garlic cloves, crushed
1 red onion, halved and sliced
3 mixed bell peppers, seeded and diced
3 cups sliced button mushrooms
2 celery stalks, sliced
1 zucchini, diced
½ teaspoon chili powder
½ teaspoon ground cumin
2 tomatoes, chopped
1¼ cups tomato paste
3 tablespoons chopped fresh basil
8 dried oven-ready lasagna noodles
salt and pepper

cheese sauce
2 tablespoons butter
1 tablespoon all-purpose flour
⅔ cup vegetable stock
1¼ cups whole milk
⅔ cup shredded vegetarian cheddar cheese
1 teaspoon Dijon mustard
1 egg, beaten

1. Place the eggplant slices in a colander, sprinkle with salt, and let stand for 20 minutes. Rinse under cold water, drain, and reserve.

2. Preheat the oven to 350°F. Heat the oil in a saucepan. Add the garlic and onion and sauté for 1–2 minutes. Add the bell peppers, mushrooms, celery, and zucchini and cook, stirring continuously, for 3–4 minutes.

3. Stir in the chili powder and cumin and cook for 1 minute. Mix in the tomatoes, tomato paste, and 2 tablespoons of the basil and season with salt and pepper.

4. For the sauce, melt the butter in a saucepan. Stir in the flour and cook for 1 minute. Remove from the heat, gradually stir in the stock and milk, return to the heat, then add half the cheese and all the mustard. Boil, stirring, until thickened. Stir in the remaining basil. Remove from the heat and stir in the egg.

5. Place half the lasagna noodles in an ovenproof dish. Top with half the vegetable and tomato sauce, then half the eggplants. Repeat and then spoon the cheese sauce on top. Sprinkle with the remaining cheese and bake in the preheated oven for 40 minutes, until golden and bubbling. Serve immediately.

Pasta with Leek & Butternut Squash

 SERVES 4   PREP TIME: 15 minutes   COOKING TIME: 40 minutes

nutritional information per serving	334 cal, 5g fat, 1.5g sat fat, 9g total sugars, 0.4g salt

This unusual dish combines the sweetness of roasted vegetables with warm spice and aromatic cilantro.

INGREDIENTS

2 cups ¾-inch baby leeks slices
1½ cups butternut squash chunks
1½ tablespoons medium curry paste
1 teaspoon vegetable oil
10 cherry tomatoes
8 ounces dried farfalle (pasta bow ties)
2 tablespoons chopped fresh cilantro
salt

white sauce
1 cup skim milk
3 tablespoons cornstarch
1 teaspoon dry mustard
1 small onion, left whole
2 small bay leaves
4 teaspoons grated vegetarian Parmesan-style cheese

1. To make the white sauce, put the milk into a saucepan with the cornstarch, dry mustard, onion, and bay leaves. Beat over medium heat until thick. Remove from the heat, discard the onion and bay leaves, and stir in the cheese. Set aside, stirring occasionally to prevent a skin from forming. Preheat the oven to 400°F.

2. Bring a large saucepan of water to a boil, add the leeks, and cook for 2 minutes. Add the butternut squash and cook for an additional 2 minutes. Drain in a colander. Mix the curry paste with the oil in a large bowl. Toss the leeks and butternut squash in the mixture to coat thoroughly.

3. Transfer the leeks and squash to a nonstick baking sheet and roast in the preheated oven for 10 minutes, until golden brown. Add the tomatoes and roast for an additional 5 minutes.

4. Meanwhile, bring a large saucepan of lightly salted water to a boil. Add the pasta, bring back to a boil, and cook for 8–10 minutes, or according to the package directions, until tender but still firm to the bite. Drain well. Put the white sauce into a large saucepan and warm over low heat. Add the leeks, squash, tomatoes, and cilantro and stir in the pasta. Transfer to warm plates and serve immediately.

Mushroom Cannelloni

 SERVES 4

 PREP TIME:
15 minutes

COOKING TIME:
50 minutes

nutritional information
per serving | 866 cal, 51g fat, 16g sat fat, 13g total sugars, 1.5g salt

This dish is perfect for mushroom lovers. You can use any combination of wild mushrooms you prefer. Porcini, in particular, add an extra strong and nutty flavor.

INGREDIENTS

12 dried cannelloni tubes

⅓ cup olive oil, plus extra for brushing

1 onion, finely chopped

2 garlic cloves, finely chopped

1 (28-ounce) can diced tomatoes

1 tablespoon tomato paste

8 ripe black olives, pitted and chopped

2 tablespoons butter

1 pound wild mushrooms, chopped

2 cups fresh bread crumbs

⅔ cup whole milk

1 cup vegetarian ricotta cheese

⅓ cup freshly grated vegetarian Parmesan-style cheese

2 tablespoons pine nuts

2 tablespoons slivered almonds

salt and pepper

1. Preheat the oven to 375°F. Bring a large saucepan of lightly salted water to a boil. Add the cannelloni tubes, return to a boil, and cook for 8–10 minutes, or until tender but still firm to the bite. With a slotted spoon, transfer the cannelloni tubes to a plate and pat dry. Brush a large ovenproof dish with oil.

2. Heat 2 tablespoons of the oil in a skillet, add the onion and half the garlic, and cook over low heat for 5 minutes, or until softened. Add the tomatoes and their can juices, tomato paste, and olives and season with salt and pepper. Bring to a boil and cook for 3–4 minutes. Pour the sauce into the ovenproof dish.

3. To make the filling, melt the butter in a heavy skillet. Add the mushrooms and remaining garlic and cook over medium heat, stirring frequently, for 3–5 minutes, or until tender.

4. Remove the skillet from the heat. Mix together the bread crumbs, milk, and remaining oil in a large bowl, then stir in the ricotta, the mushroom mixture, and ¼ cup of the Parmesan-style cheese. Season with salt and pepper.

5. Fill the cannelloni tubes with the mushroom mixture and place them in the prepared dish. Brush with oil and sprinkle with the remaining Parmesan-style cheese, the pine nuts, and almonds. Bake in the preheated oven for 25 minutes, until golden and bubbling. Serve immediately.

Hearty Bean & Pasta Soup

 SERVES 4   PREP TIME: 10 minutes   COOKING TIME: 40 minutes

nutritional information per serving	456 cal, 16g fat, 4g sat fat, 8g total sugars, 1.3g salt

Add a little Tuscan sunshine to your dinner table with this colorful and satisfying traditional soup.

INGREDIENTS

¼ cup olive oil

1 onion, finely chopped

1 celery stalk, finely chopped

1 carrot, diced

1 bay leaf

5 cups vegetable stock

1 (14½-ounce) can diced tomatoes

6 ounces dried farfalle

1 (15-ounce) can cannellini beans, drained and rinsed

7 ounces spinach or Swiss chard, thick stems removed and shredded

salt and pepper

½ cup finely grated vegetarian Parmesan-style cheese, to serve

1. Heat the oil in a large, heavy saucepan. Add the onion, celery, and carrot and cook over medium heat for 10 minutes, stirring occasionally, until the vegetables are slightly soft. Add the bay leaf, stock, and tomatoes, then bring to a boil.

2. Reduce the heat, cover, and simmer for 15 minutes, or until the vegetables are just tender. Add the pasta and beans, bring back to a boil, and cook for 8–10 minutes, or according to package directions, until the pasta is tender but still firm to the bite.

3. Stir occasionally to prevent the pasta from sticking to the bottom of the pan and burning. Season with salt and pepper, add the spinach, and cook for an additional 2 minutes, or until tender. Remove and discard the bay leaf. Ladle the soup into warm bowls and serve immediately with grated Parmesan-style cheese.

Pappardelle with Cherry Tomatoes, Arugula & Mozzarella

 SERVES 4   PREP TIME: 5 minutes   COOKING TIME: 15 minutes

nutritional information per serving	1,218 cal, 46g fat, 23g sat fat, 10g total sugars, 1.6g salt

Creamy cheese, pungent leaves, and sweet tomatoes are a great combination that tastes as good as it looks.

INGREDIENTS

1 pound dried pappardelle
2 tablespoons olive oil
1 garlic clove, chopped
2½ cups halved cherry tomatoes
5 cups arugula leaves
2 cups chopped vegetarian mozzarella
salt and pepper
grated vegetarian Parmesan-style cheese, to serve

1. Bring a large saucepan of lightly salted water to a boil. Add the pasta, bring back to a boil, and cook for 8–10 minutes, or according to the package directions, until tender but still firm to the bite.

2. Meanwhile, heat the oil in a skillet over medium heat and sauté the garlic, stirring, for 1 minute, without browning.

3. Add the tomatoes, season well with salt and pepper, and cook gently for 2–3 minutes, until softened.

4. Drain the pasta and stir into the skillet. Add the arugula leaves and mozzarella, then stir until the leaves wilt.

5. Serve the pasta in warm dishes, sprinkled with the vegetarian Parmesan-style cheese.

GOES WELL WITH
While not a traditional Italian accompaniment, rye bread is a good choice to serve with this flavorsome dish.

Spaghetti with Meat Sauce *38*

Turkey Pasta Casserole *40*

Lasagna al Forno *42*

Farfalle with Chicken & Broccoli *44*

Pasta with Chicken & Bell Peppers *46*

Pepperoni Pasta *48*

Spaghetti & Corned Beef *50*

Hamburger Pasta *52*

Spaghetti with Bacon & Crispy Bread Crumbs *54*

Pasta with Harissa Turkey Meatballs *56*

Penne Pasta with Sausage *58*

Spaghetti Carbonara *60*

Pasta with Bacon & Tomatoes *62*

Chicken with Creamy Penne *64*

Meat & Poultry

Spaghetti with Meat Sauce

SERVES 4   PREP TIME: COOKING TIME:
                15 minutes   40 minutes

nutritional information per serving	535 cal, 14g fat, 4g sat fat, 5g total sugars, 0.4g salt

This classic meat sauce (ragù) from Bologna can also be made with ground veal or half beef and half pork.

INGREDIENTS

12 ounces spaghetti or pasta of your choice

fresh Parmesan cheese shavings, to garnish (optional)

sprigs of thyme, to garnish

crusty bread, to serve

meat sauce
2 tablespoons olive oil

1 onion, finely chopped

2 garlic cloves, finely chopped

1 carrot, finely chopped

1 cup quartered white button mushrooms (optional)

1 teaspoon dried oregano

½ teaspoon dried thyme

1 bay leaf

10 ounces lean ground beef

1¼ cups stock

1¼ cups tomato puree

pepper

1. To make the sauce, heat the oil in a heavy, nonstick saucepan. Add the onion and sauté, half covered, for 5 minutes, or until soft. Add the garlic, carrot, and mushrooms, if using, and sauté for an additional 3 minutes, stirring occasionally.

2. Add the herbs and ground beef to the pan and cook until the meat has browned, stirring regularly.

3. Add the stock and tomato puree. Reduce the heat, season with pepper, and cook over medium–low heat, half covered, for 15–20 minutes, or until the sauce has reduced and thickened. Remove and discard the bay leaf.

4. Meanwhile, bring a large saucepan of lightly salted water to a boil. Add the pasta, bring back to a boil, and cook for 8–10 minutes, or according to the package directions, until tender but still firm to the bite. Drain well and mix together the pasta and sauce until the pasta is well coated. Garnish with the Parmesan cheese, if using, and sprigs of thyme. Serve immediately, with the crusty bread.

Turkey Pasta Casserole

 SERVES 4   PREP TIME: 15 minutes   COOKING TIME: 50 minutes

nutritional information per serving	614 cal, 27g fat, 15g sat fat, 8g total sugars, 1.1g salt

This fail-safe casserole is filling, easy to make, and economical—perfect for a midweek family dinner.

INGREDIENTS

1 stick butter
1 tablespoon olive oil
1 onion, finely chopped
1 pound fresh ground turkey
2 tablespoons all-purpose flour
3 cups whole milk
1 teaspoon Dijon mustard
¾ cup shredded cheddar cheese
10 ounces dried macaroni
2 tablespoons chopped fresh parsley
2 cups fresh bread crumbs

1. Melt 2 tablespoons of the butter with the oil in a skillet. Add the onion and cook over low heat, stirring occasionally, for 5 minutes, until soft. Add the turkey, increase the heat to medium, and cook, stirring frequently, for 7–8 minutes, until evenly browned. Remove the skillet from the heat, transfer the turkey and onion to a bowl with a slotted spoon, and set aside.

2. Melt 3 tablespoons of the remaining butter in a saucepan, stir in the flour, and cook, stirring continuously, for 1 minute. Remove the pan from the heat and gradually beat in the milk, then return to the heat and bring to a boil, beating continuously until thickened. Remove the pan from the heat and stir in the mustard, turkey mixture, and ½ cup of the cheese.

3. Preheat the oven to 350°F. Bring a large saucepan of lightly salted water to a boil. Add the pasta, bring back to a boil, and cook for 8–10 minutes, or according to the package directions, until tender but still firm to the bite. Drain and stir into the turkey mixture with the parsley.

4. Spoon the mixture into an ovenproof dish, sprinkle with the bread crumbs and remaining cheese, and dot with the remaining butter. Bake in the preheated oven for 25 minutes, until golden and bubbling. Serve immediately.

Lasagna al Forno

 SERVES 6

PREP TIME:
15 minutes

COOKING TIME:
2¼ hours

nutritional information per serving	629 cal, 71g fat, 30g sat fat, 5g total sugars, 2.8g salt

You need plenty of time to make a baked lasagna with an authentic flavor, but it is worth it.

INGREDIENTS

¾ cup olive oil

4 tablespoons butter

4 ounces pancetta

1 onion, finely chopped

1 celery stalk, finely chopped

1 carrot, finely chopped

12 ounces chuck steak, in a single piece

⅓ cup red wine

2 tablespoons tomato paste

8 ounces Italian link sausages

2 eggs

1¾ cups freshly grated Parmesan cheese

⅔ cup fresh bread crumbs

1⅓ cups ricotta cheese

8 dried oven-ready lasagna noodles

12 ounces mozzarella cheese, sliced

salt and pepper

chopped fresh parsley, to garnish

1. Heat ½ cup of the oil with the butter in a large saucepan. Add the pancetta, onion, celery, and carrot and cook over low heat, until soft. Increase the heat to medium, add the steak, and cook until evenly browned. Stir in the wine and tomato paste, season with salt and pepper, and bring to a boil. Reduce the heat, cover, and simmer gently for 1½ hours, until the steak is tender.

2. Meanwhile, heat 2 tablespoons of the remaining oil in a skillet. Add the sausage and cook for 8–10 minutes. Remove from the skillet and discard the skin. Thinly slice the sausage and set aside. Transfer the steak to a cutting board and finely dice. Return half the steak to the sauce.

3. Mix the remaining steak in a bowl with 1 egg, 1 tablespoon of the Parmesan cheese, and the bread crumbs. Shape into walnut-size balls. Heat the remaining oil in a skillet, add the meatballs, and cook for 5–8 minutes, until brown. Pass the ricotta through a strainer into a bowl. Stir in the remaining egg and ¼ cup of the remaining Parmesan cheese.

4. Preheat the oven to 350°F. In a rectangular ovenproof dish, make layers with the lasagna noodles, ricotta mixture, meat sauce, meatballs, sausage, and mozzarella cheese. Finish with a layer of the ricotta mixture and sprinkle with the remaining Parmesan cheese.

5. Bake the lasagna in the preheated oven for 20–25 minutes, until golden and bubbling. Serve immediately, garnished with chopped parsley.

Farfalle with Chicken & Broccoli

 SERVES 4   PREP TIME: 10 minutes   COOKING TIME: 20–25 minutes

nutritional information per serving	707 cal, 33g fat, 12g sat fat, 3g total sugars, 0.7g salt

This is one of those dishes that looks almost too pretty to eat, but it's far too tasty to resist.

INGREDIENTS

¼ cup olive oil

5 tablespoons butter

3 garlic cloves, minced

1 pound skinless, boneless chicken breasts, diced

¼ teaspoon crushed red pepper flakes

6 cups small broccoli florets (about 1 pound)

10½ ounces dried farfalle (pasta bow ties)

1 (7-ounce) jar roasted red peppers, drained and diced

1¼ cups chicken stock

salt and pepper

1. Bring a large saucepan of lightly salted water to a boil. Meanwhile, heat the oil and butter in a large skillet over a medium–low heat and cook the garlic until just beginning to brown.

2. Add the diced chicken, increase the heat to medium, and cook for 4–5 minutes, until the chicken is cooked through. Add the crushed red pepper and season with salt and pepper. Remove from the heat.

3. Plunge the broccoli into the boiling water and cook for 2 minutes. Remove with a slotted spoon and set aside. Bring the water back to a boil. Add the pasta and cook for 8–10 minutes, or according to the package directions, until tender but still firm to the bite. Drain thoroughly and add to the chicken mixture in the skillet. Add the broccoli and roasted peppers. Pour in the stock. Simmer briskly over medium–high heat, stirring frequently, until most of the liquid has been absorbed.

4. Transfer to warm dishes and serve immediately.

1

2

3

GOES WELL WITH
The perfect accompaniment would be a light rosé wine or, if you prefer a non-alcoholic drink, sparkling grape or apple juice.

Pasta with Chicken & Bell Peppers

 SERVES 4

PREP TIME:
25 minutes
plus marinating

COOKING TIME:
40 minutes

nutritional information per serving	500 cal, 11g fat, 2g sat fat, 8g total sugars, 0.4g salt

You have to allow time for the chicken to marinate, but this mouthwatering spicy dish is worth the wait.

INGREDIENTS

12 skinless, boneless chicken thighs, cubed

1 tablespoon peanut oil

1 red bell pepper, seeded and chopped

1 green bell pepper, seeded and chopped

1 cup canned diced tomatoes

1 pound dried spaghetti

salt

marinade

2 tablespoons finely chopped scallions, plus extra to garnish

1–2 chiles, seeded and chopped

2 garlic cloves, finely chopped

1 teaspoon ground cinnamon

1 teaspoon ground allspice

pinch of grated nutmeg

2 teaspoons light brown sugar

2 tablespoons peanut oil

1 tablespoon lime juice

1 tablespoon white wine vinegar

salt and pepper

1. Put the chicken into a large, nonmetallic dish. Mix all the marinade ingredients in a bowl, mashing everything together. Spoon the mixture over the chicken and rub it in with your hands. Cover the dish with plastic wrap and let marinate in the refrigerator for at least 2 hours, preferably overnight.

2. Heat the oil in a saucepan, add the red and green bell peppers, and cook over medium–low heat, stirring occasionally, for 5 minutes. Add the chicken and marinade and cook, stirring frequently, for 5 minutes, until cooked through. Add the tomatoes, reduce the heat, cover, and simmer, stirring occasionally, for 30 minutes. Check occasionally that the mixture is not drying out—if it is, add a little water.

3. Halfway through the chicken cooking time, bring a large saucepan of lightly salted water to a boil. Add the pasta, bring back to a boil, and cook for 8–10 minutes, or according to the package directions, until tender but still firm to the bite.

4. Drain the pasta, add it to the pan with the chicken and toss lightly. Transfer to warm plates, garnish with the scallions, and serve immediately.

Pepperoni Pasta

 SERVES 4   PREP TIME: 10 minutes   COOKING TIME: 20 minutes

nutritional information
per serving

780 cal, 33g fat, 10g sat fat, 14g total sugars, 2.8g salt

A sure-fire favorite, this colorful and delicious dish will brighten up even a truly dull day.

INGREDIENTS

3 tablespoons olive oil

1 onion, chopped

1 red bell pepper, seeded and diced

1 orange bell pepper, seeded and diced

1 (28-ounce) can diced tomatoes

1 tablespoon tomato paste

1 teaspoon paprika

8 ounces pepperoni sausage, sliced

2 tablespoons chopped fresh flat-leaf parsley, plus extra to garnish

1 pound dried penne

salt and pepper

1. Heat 2 tablespoons of the oil in a large, heavy skillet. Add the onion and cook over low heat, stirring occasionally, for 5 minutes, or until softened. Add the red and orange bell peppers, tomatoes and their can juices, tomato paste, and paprika and bring to a boil.

2. Add the pepperoni and parsley and season with salt and pepper. Stir well, bring to a boil, then reduce the heat and simmer for 10–15 minutes.

3. Meanwhile, bring a large saucepan of lightly salted water to a boil. Add the pasta, bring back to a boil, and cook for 8–10 minutes, or according to the package directions, until tender but still firm to the bite. Drain well and transfer to a warm serving dish. Add the remaining olive oil and toss. Add the sauce and toss again. Sprinkle with parsley and serve immediately.

COOKS NOTE
Pepperoni is a hot,
spicy Italian
sausage made
from pork and
beef and flavored
with fennel. You
could substitute
another spicy
sausage, such
as chorizo.

Spaghetti & Corned Beef

SERVES 4

PREP TIME:
15 minutes

COOKING TIME:
25–30 minutes

nutritional information
per serving — 742 cal, 21g fat, 8g sat fat, 8g total sugars, 2.8g salt

This variation of corned beef and hash will be popular with children and is also economical, and it is an easy way to make a change in the normal family menu.

INGREDIENTS

2 tablespoons sunflower oil

1 large onion, chopped

2–3 garlic cloves, finely chopped

1 pound corned beef, chopped

1 (14½-ounce) can diced tomatoes

1 pound dried spaghetti

2 tablespoons chopped fresh parsley

pinch of crushed red pepper flakes or dash of Tabasco sauce or Worcestershire sauce

salt and pepper

1. Heat the oil in a large skillet, add the onion and garlic, and cook over medium heat for 5 minutes, until just beginning to brown.

2. Add the corned beef and cook, stirring and mashing with a wooden spoon, for 5–8 minutes, until it is dry. Drain the tomatoes, reserving the can juices, and stir them into the skillet. Cook for an additional 10 minutes, adding a little of the reserved can juices if the mixture seems to be drying out too much.

3. Meanwhile, bring a large saucepan of lightly salted water to a boil. Add the pasta, bring back to a boil, and cook for 8–10 minutes, or according to the package directions, until tender but still firm to the bite.

4. Drain the pasta and add it to the skillet. Stir in the parsley and crushed red pepper and season with salt and pepper, keeping in mind that corned beef is often already salty. Mix well and heat through for an additional few minutes. Serve immediately.

1

2

2

HEALTHY HINT
You can buy cans
of reduced-salt
corned beef if you
are concerned about
the levels of salt
in your diet.

Hamburger Pasta

SERVES 4

PREP TIME:
10 minutes

COOKING TIME:
15 minutes

nutritional information per serving	686 cal, 34g fat, 12g sat fat, 8g total sugars, 0.9g salt

This is a good way to use up extra hamburger patties, combining them with staple ingredients for a quick meal.

INGREDIENTS

10 ounces dried conchiglie (pasta shells)

12 ounces hamburger patties

1 (16-ounce) package frozen mixed vegetables, such as carrots, corn, and broccoli or green beans

1 (14½-ounce) can tomatoes, drained

1 garlic clove, finely chopped

1–1½ pickled jalapeño chiles, finely chopped

3 tablespoons olive oil

2 tablespoons freshly grated Parmesan cheese

salt and pepper

1. Preheat the broiler. Bring a large saucepan of lightly salted water to a boil. Add the pasta, bring back to a boil, and cook for 8–10 minutes, or according to the package directions, until tender but still firm to the bite.

2. Meanwhile, cook the hamburger patties under the preheated broiler for 7–8 minutes on each side until cooked through. Meanwhile, bring a separate saucepan of lightly salted water to a boil, add the frozen vegetables, and cook for about 5 minutes.

3. Drain the vegetables, transfer to a food processor, and process briefly until chopped, then put into a saucepan. Transfer the cooked burgers to the food processor and process briefly until chopped, then add to the pan of vegetables. Stir in the tomatoes, garlic, chiles, and oil, season with salt and pepper, and reheat gently.

4. Drain the pasta and put it into a warm serving bowl. Add the burger-and-vegetable mixture and toss lightly. Sprinkle with the cheese and serve immediately.

3

3

3

SOMETHING
DIFFERENT
If serving to young
children or if you
just don't like spicy
food, omit the chiles
and add a pinch of
dried oregano instead.

Spaghetti with Bacon & Crispy Bread Crumbs

SERVES 2

PREP TIME:
10 minutes

COOKING TIME:
10 minutes

nutritional information per serving	787 cal, 42g fat, 11g sat fat, 4g total sugars, 2.7g salt

Quick, easy, and economical, yet truly mouthwatering, this is the perfect midweek home-from-work supper.

INGREDIENTS

1 day-old ciabatta roll
sprig of fresh rosemary
6 ounces dried spaghetti
2 teaspoons olive oil
5 ounces smoked bacon, chopped
1 tablespoon butter
⅓ cup pine nuts
2 garlic cloves, crushed
2–3 tablespoons chopped fresh flat-leaf parsley
salt and pepper

1. Put the day-old bread, including any crusts, in a food processor or blender and process until the mixture resembles coarse bread crumbs. Bruise the rosemary sprig in a mortar and pestle or use a rolling pin to release the flavor.

2. Bring a large saucepan of lightly salted water to a boil. Add the pasta, bring back to a boil, and cook for 8–10 minutes, or according to the package directions, until tender but still firm to the bite.

3. Meanwhile, heat the oil in a large skillet, add the bacon and rosemary, and sauté for 2–3 minutes, until the bacon is golden brown. Transfer to a warm serving bowl using a slotted spoon.

4. Add the butter to the bacon fat remaining in the skillet. When melted and foaming, add the bread crumbs, pine nuts, and garlic. Sauté for 2–3 minutes, stirring until golden brown, then put into the bowl with the bacon.

5. Drain the pasta and transfer to the bowl with the bacon and bread crumbs. Add the parsley, season with pepper, and toss well. Serve immediately.

Pasta with Harissa Turkey Meatballs

 SERVES 4

PREP TIME: 15 minutes

COOKING TIME: 15–20 minutes

nutritional information per serving	560 cal, 10g fat, 3g sat fat, 7.5g total sugars, 0.7g salt

If you like spicy food, this North African-style dish is the perfect choice, and you can easily adjust the heat to suit you.

INGREDIENTS

12 ounces fresh ground turkey

½ cup dry bread crumbs

⅓ cup Greek-style yogurt

1 egg

½ teaspoon ground coriander

½ teaspoon ground cumin

½–1 teaspoon harissa

3 tablespoons finely chopped fresh parsley

12 ounces dried spaghetti or tagliatelle

olive oil, for drizzling

salt and pepper

sauce

1 (14½-ounce) can diced tomatoes

1 small chile, seeded and finely chopped

¼ teaspoon ground cinnamon

½ teaspoon ground cumin

1. Preheat the oven to 400°F and line a baking sheet with parchment paper.

2. Mix together the turkey, bread crumbs, yogurt, egg, coriander, cumin, harissa, and parsley in a bowl until thoroughly combined. Season with salt and pepper. Shape the mixture into meatballs about the size of a golf ball and put them on the prepared baking sheet. Bake for 15 minutes, until lightly browned.

3. Meanwhile, bring a large saucepan of lightly salted water to a boil. Add the pasta, bring back to a boil, and cook for 8–10 minutes, or according to the package directions, until tender but still firm to the bite.

4. Meanwhile, put all the sauce ingredients into a saucepan and simmer, stirring occasionally, for 5 minutes, until thickened. Drain the pasta, transfer to a warm dish, drizzle with oil, and toss to coat.

5. Remove the meatballs from the oven and add to the pasta. Pour the sauce over them and toss together. Serve immediately.

Penne Pasta with Sausage

 SERVES 6

PREP TIME:
15 minutes

COOKING TIME:
20–25 minutes

nutritional information per serving	437 cal, 19g fat, 6g sat fat, 5g total sugars, 1.5g salt

Packed with flavor and lively rather than fiery, this is an ideal dish for informal entertaining.

INGREDIENTS

2 tablespoons olive oil

1 red onion, coarsely chopped

2 garlic cloves, coarsely chopped

6 Italian link sausages, skinned and the meat crumbled

½ teaspoon crushed red pepper flakes

2 tablespoons chopped fresh oregano

1 (14½-ounce) can diced tomatoes

12 ounces dried penne

salt and pepper

1. Heat the oil in a large saucepan, add the onion, and cook over medium heat, stirring frequently, for 6–8 minutes, until starting to brown. Add the garlic and the crumbled sausages and cook for 8–10 minutes, breaking up the sausages with a wooden spoon.

2. Add the crushed red pepper and oregano and stir well. Pour in the tomatoes and bring to a boil. Place over low heat and simmer for 4–5 minutes, until reduced and thickened. Season with salt and pepper.

3. Meanwhile, bring a large saucepan of lightly salted water to a boil. Add the pasta, bring back to a boil, and cook for 8–10 minutes, or according to the package directions, until tender but still firm to the bite. Drain thoroughly and return to the pan.

4. Pour the sauce into the pasta and stir well. Transfer to warm serving plates and serve immediately.

1

2

3
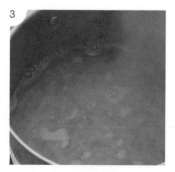

COOK'S NOTE

Italian link-style sausages are popular for their spicy flavor. However, if you can't find them, use any good-quality pork link sausages instead.

Spaghetti Carbonara

 SERVES 4

PREP TIME: 15 minutes

COOKING TIME: 15–20 minutes

nutritional information per serving	1,498 cal, 73g fat, 35g sat fat, 7g total sugars, 4g salt

This popular Italian dish combines pancetta and heavy cream with two hard cheeses—Parmesan and pecorino.

INGREDIENTS

1 pound dried spaghetti

4 eggs

¼ cup heavy cream

⅔ cup grated Parmesan cheese, plus extra to garnish

⅔ cup grated pecorino cheese

1 tablespoon butter

6 ounces pancetta, finely diced

salt and pepper

1. Bring a large saucepan of lightly salted water to a boil. Add the pasta, bring back to a boil, and cook for 8–10 minutes, or according to the package directions, until tender but still firm to the bite.

2. Meanwhile, stir together the eggs, cream, Parmesan cheese, and pecorino cheese in a bowl. Season with salt and pepper.

3. Melt the butter in a large saucepan, add the pancetta, and cook over medium heat for 8-10 minutes, until crispy. Drain the spaghetti and add it to the pan while still dripping wet. Pour the cheese sauce over spaghetti. Remove the pan from the heat. Toss the spaghetti in the sauce until the eggs begin to thicken but are still creamy.

4. Transfer to warm plates and serve immediately, sprinkled with pepper and a little more Parmesan cheese.

2 3 3

COOK'S NOTE
For a more substantial dish, cook 1-2 finely chopped shallots with the pancetta and add 2 cups sliced button mushrooms.

Pasta with Bacon & Tomatoes

 SERVES 4 | PREP TIME: 15 minutes | COOKING TIME: 25–30 minutes

nutritional information per serving	592 cal, 17g fat, 8g sat fat, 10g total sugars, 1.5g salt

This is an ideal dish to serve in the summer, when tomatoes are at their sweetest.

INGREDIENTS

10 small, sweet tomatoes (about 2 pounds)

6 rindless smoked bacon strips

4 tablespoons butter

1 onion, chopped

1 garlic clove, crushed

4 fresh oregano sprigs, finely chopped

1 pound dried orecchiette ("little ears") pasta

salt and pepper

freshly grated pecorino cheese, to serve

1. Blanch the tomatoes in boiling water. Drain, peel, and seed the tomatoes, then coarsely chop the flesh.

2. Using a sharp knife, chop the bacon into small dice. Melt the butter in a saucepan. Add the bacon and cook for 2-3 minutes, until golden brown.

3. Add the onion and garlic and cook over medium heat for 5–7 minutes, until just softened. Add the tomatoes and oregano to the pan, then season with salt and pepper. Lower the heat and simmer for 10–12 minutes.

4. Meanwhile, bring a large saucepan of lightly salted water to a boil. Add the pasta, bring back to a boil, and cook for 8–10 minutes, or according to the package directions, until tender but still firm to the bite. Drain the pasta and transfer to a warm serving bowl. Spoon the bacon-and-tomato sauce over the pasta, toss to coat, and serve immediately with the pecorino cheese.

1

3

4

Chicken with Creamy Penne

 SERVES 2

PREP TIME:
5 minutes

COOKING TIME:
10–15 minutes

nutritional information per serving	810 cal, 30g fat, 15g sat fat, 4g total sugars, 0.3g salt

It is the pure simplicity of this delicately flavored dish that makes it absolutely perfect.

INGREDIENTS

8 ounces dried penne
1 tablespoon olive oil
2 skinless, boneless chicken breasts
¼ cup dry white wine
¾ cup frozen peas
⅓ cup heavy cream
¼ cup chopped fresh parsley, to garnish

1. Bring a large saucepan of lightly salted water to a boil. Add the pasta, bring back to a boil, and cook for 8–10 minutes, or according to the package directions, until tender but still firm to the bite.

2. Meanwhile, heat the oil in a skillet, add the chicken, and cook over medium heat for about 4 minutes on each side, until cooked through and the juices run clear.

3. Pour in the wine and cook over high heat until it has almost evaporated.

4. Drain the pasta. Add the peas, cream, and pasta to the skillet and stir well. Cover and simmer for 2 minutes. Garnish with chopped parsley and serve immediately.

GOES WELL WITH
A colorful endive,
orange, and beet
salad with a yogurt
dressing makes the
perfect partner for
this creamy dish.

Tuna Noodle Casserole *68*

Spaghetti & Cod *70*

Sicilian Swordfish Pasta *72*

Linguine with Clams in Tomato Sauce *74*

Tagliatelle with Smoked Salmon & Arugula *76*

Penne with Squid & Tomatoes *78*

Pasta Salad with Melon & Shrimp *80*

Salmon Lasagna Rolls *82*

Spaghetti with Tuna & Parsley *84*

Linguine with Shrimp & Scallops *86*

Spaghetti with Tuna Sauce *88*

Salad Niçoise *90*

Scallop Soup with Pasta *92*

Mussel & Pasta Soup *94*

Fish & Seafood

Tuna Noodle Casserole

 SERVES 4

 PREP TIME:
20 minutes

 COOKING TIME:
35 minutes

nutritional information per serving	600 cal, 27g fat, 13g sat fat, 8g total sugars, 2.6g salt

Ever since canned condensed soups were invented in 1897, they have been used in casserole cooking. The most popular of these meals continues to be tuna noodle casserole.

INGREDIENTS

8 ounces dried tagliatelle

2 tablespoons butter

1¼ cups fresh bread crumbs

1 (14½-ounce) can condensed cream of mushroom soup

½ cup whole milk

2 celery stalks, chopped

1 red and 1 green bell pepper, seeded and chopped

1¼ cups shredded sharp cheddar cheese

2 tablespoons chopped fresh parsley

1 (5-ounce) can chunk light tuna in oil, drained and flaked

salt and pepper

1. Preheat the oven to 400°F. Bring a large saucepan of lightly salted water to a boil. Add the pasta and cook for 2 minutes less than the time specified in the package directions.

2. Meanwhile, melt the butter in a separate small saucepan over medium heat. Stir in the bread crumbs, then remove from the heat and reserve.

3. Drain the pasta thoroughly and reserve. Pour the soup into the pasta pan over medium heat, then stir in the milk, celery, bell peppers, half the cheese, and all the parsley. Add the tuna and gently stir in so that the flakes don't break up. Season with salt and pepper. Heat just until small bubbles appear around the edge of the mixture—do not boil.

4. Stir the pasta into the pan and use two forks to mix together all the ingredients. Spoon the mixture into an ovenproof dish and spread out. Stir the remaining cheese into the buttered bread crumbs, then sprinkle over the top of the pasta mixture. Bake in the preheated oven for 20–25 minutes, until golden and bubbling. Let stand for 5 minutes before serving.

Spaghetti & Cod

 SERVES 4   PREP TIME: 10 minutes   COOKING TIME: 12 minutes

nutritional information per serving	725 cal, 39g fat, 6g sat fat, 6g total sugars, 0.3g salt

This recipe is incredibly quick and easy to prepare, and the dish is surprisingly tasty.

INGREDIENTS

10 ounces dried spaghetti

1 cup extra virgin olive oil

1 garlic clove, peeled and kept whole

3 cups halved cherry tomatoes

pinch of crushed red peppers flakes (optional)

1¼ pounds cod fillets, skinned and cut into small chunks

salt and pepper

1. Bring a large saucepan of lightly salted water to a boil. Add the pasta, bring back to a boil, and cook for 8–10 minutes, or according to the package directions, until tender but still firm to the bite.

2. Meanwhile, put the oil into a large saucepan, add the garlic, and cook over low heat, stirring occasionally, for a few minutes, until the garlic starts to brown, then remove and discard. Add the tomatoes to the pan and season with salt. Increase the heat to high and cook, tossing occasionally, for 6–7 minutes, until lightly browned and concentrated without disintegrating.

3. Add the crushed red peppers, if using, and the fish and cook, stirring gently, for 1–2 minutes. Add a ladleful of the cooking water from the pasta and taste and adjust the seasoning, if necessary. Drain the pasta, add it to the sauce, and toss together. Remove from the heat, spoon into warm bowls, and serve immediately.

SOMETHING
DIFFERENT
You can substitute
another firm-
fleshed white fish,
such as halibut or
red snapper for
the cod.

Sicilian Swordfish Pasta

nutritional information per serving	441 cal, 10g fat, 2g sat fat, 6.5g total sugars, 1.1g salt

Sicily is famous for its swordfish recipes, which often also include other favorite ingredients, such as capers and olives.

INGREDIENTS

1 tablespoon olive oil

4 garlic cloves, peeled

1 onion, chopped

8 ripe black olives, pitted and chopped

4 small pickles, chopped

2 tablespoons capers in salt, rinsed and chopped

10 ounces dried spaghetti or linguine

1 (14½-ounce) can diced tomatoes

1 pound swordfish, cut into small chunks

salt and pepper

basil leaves, to garnish

1. Heat the oil in a deep skillet and add the garlic. When the garlic begins to brown, remove and discard. Add the onion and cook over low heat, stirring occasionally, for 8–10 minutes, until light golden. Stir in the olives, pickles, and capers, season with salt and pepper, and cook, stirring occasionally, for 5 minutes.

2. Meanwhile, bring a large saucepan of lightly salted water to a boil. Add the pasta, bring back to a boil, and cook for 8–10 minutes, or according to the package directions, until tender but still firm to the bite.

3. Add the tomatoes to the skillet, increase the heat to medium, and bring to a boil, stirring occasionally, then reduce the heat and simmer for 5 minutes. Add the swordfish chunks, cover, and simmer gently for an additional 5 minutes.

4. Drain the pasta and transfer to a warm serving dish. Top with the swordfish sauce, sprinkle the basil leaves over the fish, and serve immediately.

1

1

3

COOK'S NOTE
Although it's
an oily fish,
swordfish dries
out easily, so
simmer until it is
just opaque to avoid
overcooking.

Linguine with Clams in Tomato Sauce

 SERVES 4 · PREP TIME: 20 minutes · COOKING TIME: 35 minutes

nutritional information per serving	522 cal, 11.5g fat, 2g sat fat, 9g total sugars, 0.7g salt

This Neapolitan specialty features three of the city's favorite ingredients—pasta, tomatoes, and clams.

INGREDIENTS

2¼ pounds live clams, scrubbed
1 cup dry white wine
2 garlic cloves, coarsely chopped
¼ cup chopped fresh flat-leaf parsley
2 tablespoons olive oil
1 onion, chopped
8 plum tomatoes, peeled, seeded, and chopped
1 fresh red chile, seeded and chopped
12 ounces dried linguine
salt and pepper

1. Discard any clams with broken shells or any that refuse to close when tapped. Pour the wine into a large, heavy saucepan and add the garlic, half the parsley, and the clams. Cover and cook over high heat, shaking the pan occasionally, for 5 minutes, or until the shells have opened. Remove the clams with a slotted spoon, reserving the cooking liquid. Discard any that remain closed and remove half of the remainder from their shells. Keep the shelled and unshelled clams in separate covered bowls. Strain the cooking liquid through a cheesecloth-lined strainer and reserve.

2. Heat the oil in a heavy saucepan. Add the onion and cook over low heat for 5 minutes, or until softened. Add the tomatoes, chile, and reserved cooking liquid and season with salt and pepper. Bring to a boil, partly cover the pan, and simmer for 20 minutes.

3. Meanwhile, bring a large saucepan of lightly salted water to a boil. Add the pasta, bring back to a boil, and cook for 8–10 minutes, or according to the package directions, until tender but still firm to the bite. Drain and transfer to a warm serving dish.

4. Stir the shelled clams into the tomato sauce and heat through gently for 2–3 minutes. Pour over the pasta and toss. Garnish with the clams in their shells and remaining parsley. Serve immediately.

Tagliatelle with Smoked Salmon & Arugula

 SERVES 4   PREP TIME: 5 minutes   COOKING TIME: 15 minutes

nutritional information per serving	1,141 cal, 76g fat, 44g sat fat, 5g total sugars, 2g salt

This must be one of the easiest dishes to prepare— and one of the most delicious to eat.

INGREDIENTS

12 ounces dried tagliatelle
2 tablespoons olive oil
1 garlic clove, finely chopped
4 ounces smoked salmon, cut into thin strips
3 cups arugula
salt and pepper

1. Bring a large saucepan of lightly salted water to a boil. Add the pasta, bring back to a boil, and cook for 8–10 minutes, or according to the package directions, until tender but still firm to the bite.

2. Just before the end of the cooking time, heat the olive oil in a heavy skillet. Add the garlic and cook over low heat, stirring continuously, for 1 minute. Do not let the garlic brown or it will taste bitter.

3. Add the salmon and arugula. Season with pepper and cook, stirring continuously, for 1 minute. Remove the skillet from the heat.

4. Drain the pasta and transfer to a warm serving dish. Add the salmon and arugula mixture, toss lightly and serve immediately.

1   2   3

GOES WELL WITH
Garlic bread would
make a wonderful
complement without
detracting from the
delicate flavors
of the dish.

Penne with Squid & Tomatoes

 SERVES 4   PREP TIME: 15 minutes   COOKING TIME: 30–35 minutes

nutritional information per serving	493 cal, 19g fat, 3g sat fat, 8g total sugars, 0.6g salt

Ask your fish dealer for prepared squid to make this rich southern Italian dish quick and easy to make.

INGREDIENTS

8 ounces dried penne

12 ounces prepared squid

⅓ cup olive oil

2 onions, sliced

1 cup fish or chicken stock

⅔ cup full-bodied red wine

1 (14½-ounce) can diced tomatoes

2 tablespoons tomato paste

1 tablespoon chopped fresh marjoram

1 bay leaf

salt and pepper

2 tablespoons chopped fresh parsley, to garnish

1. Bring a large saucepan of lightly salted water to a boil. Add the pasta, bring back to a boil, and cook for 3 minutes, then drain and reserve until required. With a sharp knife, cut the squid into strips.

2. Heat the oil in a large saucepan. Add the onions and cook over low heat, stirring occasionally, for 5 minutes, or until softened. Add the squid and stock, bring to a boil, and simmer for 3 minutes. Stir in the wine, tomatoes and their can juices, tomato paste, marjoram, and bay leaf. Season with salt and pepper. Bring to a boil and cook for 5 minutes, or until slightly reduced.

3. Add the pasta, return to a boil, and simmer for 5–7 minutes, or according to the package directions, until the pasta is tender but still firm to the bite. Remove and discard the bay leaf. Transfer to a warm serving dish, garnish with the parsley, and serve immediately.

1   2   2

GOES WELL WITH
A simple salad
of mixed greens
and fresh herbs
would be a
refreshing
accompaniment
to this rich and
substantial dish.

Pasta Salad with Melon & Shrimp

 SERVES 6

PREP TIME:
25 minutes
plus chilling

COOKING TIME:
10 minutes

nutritional information per serving	334 cal, 11g fat, 1.5g sat fat, 15g total sugars, 1.2g salt

This attractive salad also has wonderful flavors, making it a great choice for a special occasion.

INGREDIENTS

8 ounces dried green fusilli (corkscrew pasta)

⅓ cup extra virgin olive oil

1 pound cooked shrimp

1 cantaloupe melon

1 honeydew melon

1 tablespoon red wine vinegar

1 teaspoon Dijon mustard

pinch of sugar

1 tablespoon chopped fresh flat-leaf parsley

1 tablespoon chopped fresh basil, plus extra sprigs to garnish

1 head of green oak-leaf lettuce or other loose-leaf lettuce, shredded

salt and pepper

1. Bring a large saucepan of lightly salted water to a boil. Add the pasta, bring back to a boil, and cook for 8–10 minutes, or according to the package directions, until tender but still firm to the bite. Drain, toss with 1 tablespoon of the oil, and let cool.

2. Meanwhile, peel and devein the shrimp, then place them in a large bowl. Halve both the melons and scoop out the seeds with a spoon. Using a melon baller or teaspoon, scoop out balls of the flesh and add them to the shrimp.

3. Beat together the remaining oil, the vinegar, mustard, sugar, parsley, and basil in a small bowl. Season with salt and pepper. Add the cooled pasta to the shrimp-and-melon mixture and toss lightly to mix, then pour in the dressing and toss again. Cover with plastic wrap and chill in the refrigerator for 30 minutes.

4. Make a bed of shredded lettuce on a serving plate. Spoon the pasta salad on top, garnish with basil sprigs, and serve immediately.

2

2

3

GOES WELL WITH
For a crunchy contrast with the ripe fruit and tender shrimp, serve with sesame seed or poppy seed grissini—Italian breadsticks.

Salmon Lasagna Rolls

 SERVES 4   PREP TIME: 15 minutes   COOKING TIME: 1 hour

nutritional information per serving	487 cal, 22g fat, 9g sat fat, 9g total sugars, 0.6g salt

This attractive and colorful dish is much easier to make than you might think and is well worth a little extra time.

INGREDIENTS

vegetable oil, for brushing
8 dried lasagna verde noodles
2 tablespoons butter
1 onion, sliced
½ red bell pepper, seeded and chopped
1 zucchini, diced
1 teaspoon chopped fresh ginger
4 ounces oyster mushrooms, torn into pieces
8 ounces salmon fillet, skinned and cut into chunks
3 tablespoons dry sherry
2 teaspoons cornstarch
3 tablespoons all-purpose flour
1¾ cups whole milk
¼ cup shredded cheddar cheese
1 tablespoon fresh white bread crumbs
salt and pepper

1. Preheat the oven to 400°F. Brush an ovenproof dish with oil. Bring a large saucepan of lightly salted water to a boil. Add the pasta, bring back to a boil, and cook for 8–10 minutes, or according to the package directions, until tender but still firm to the bite. Remove with tongs and drain on a clean dish towel.

2. Meanwhile, melt half the butter in a saucepan. Add the onion and cook over low heat, stirring occasionally, for 5 minutes, until softened. Add the red bell pepper, zucchini, and ginger and cook, stirring occasionally, for 10 minutes. Add the mushrooms and salmon and cook for 2 minutes, then mix together the sherry and cornstarch and stir into the pan. Cook for an additional 4 minutes, until the fish is opaque and flakes easily. Season with salt and pepper and remove the pan from the heat.

3. Melt the remaining butter in another pan. Stir in the flour and cook, stirring continuously, for 2 minutes. Gradually stir in the milk, then cook, stirring continuously, for 10 minutes. Remove the pan from the heat, stir in half the cheddar cheese and season with salt and pepper.

4. Spoon the salmon filling along one of the shorter sides of each lasagna noodle. Roll up and place in the prepared dish. Pour the sauce over the rolls and sprinkle with the bread crumbs and remaining cheese. Bake in the preheated oven for 15–20 minutes, until golden and bubbling. Serve immediately.

Spaghetti with Tuna & Parsley

 SERVES 4   PREP TIME: 10 minutes   COOKING TIME: 15 minutes

nutritional information per serving	1,109 cal, 70g fat, 21g sat fat, 5g total sugars, 1.6g salt

This tasty dish is a great pantry standby that can be rustled up in no time at all.

INGREDIENTS

1 pound dried spaghetti

2 tablespoons butter

1 (5-ounce) can chunk light tuna in spring water, drained

1 (2-ounce) can anchovies, drained

1¼ cups olive oil

1 large bunch of fresh flat-leaf parsley, coarsely chopped

⅔ cup crème fraîche or sour cream

salt and pepper

1. Bring a large saucepan of lightly salted water to a boil. Add the pasta, bring back to a boil, and cook for 8–10 minutes, or according to the package directions, until tender but still firm to the bite. Drain the spaghetti in a colander and return to the pan. Add the butter, toss thoroughly to coat, and keep warm until required.

2. Flake the tuna into smaller pieces using two forks. Place the tuna in a food processor or blender with the anchovies, oil, and parsley and process until the sauce is smooth. Pour in the crème fraîche and process for a few seconds to blend. Taste the sauce and season with salt and pepper, if necessary.

3. Shake the pan of spaghetti over medium heat for a few minutes, or until it is thoroughly warm.

4. Pour the sauce over the spaghetti and toss. Serve immediately.

GOES WELL WITH
A mixed bean salad, perhaps including some fresh green beans, would be a perfect match for this dish.

Linguine with Shrimp & Scallops

SERVES 6

PREP TIME: 15 minutes

COOKING TIME: 25–30 minutes

nutritional information per serving	514 cal, 10g fat, 3g sat fat, 3g total sugars, 0.8g salt

This impressive dish from the coastal regions of northern Italy is a real treat for lovers of seafood.

INGREDIENTS

1 pound shrimp

2 tablespoons butter

2 shallots, finely chopped

1 cup dry white vermouth

1½ cups water

1 pound dried linguine

2 tablespoons olive oil

1 pound prepared scallops, thawed if frozen

2 tablespoons snipped fresh chives

salt and pepper

1. Peel and devein the shrimp, reserving the shells. Melt the butter in a heavy skillet. Add the shallots and cook over low heat, stirring occasionally, for 5 minutes, or until softened. Add the shrimp shells and cook, stirring continuously, for 1 minute. Pour in the vermouth and cook, stirring, for 1 minute. Add the water, bring to a boil, then reduce the heat and simmer for 10 minutes, or until the liquid has reduced by half. Remove the skillet from the heat.

2. Bring a large saucepan of lightly salted water to a boil. Add the pasta, bring back to a boil, and cook for 8–10 minutes, or according to the package directions, until tender but still firm to the bite.

3. Meanwhile, heat the oil in a separate heavy skillet. Add the scallops and shrimp and cook, stirring frequently, for 2 minutes, or until the scallops are opaque and the shrimp have changed color. Strain the shrimp-shell stock into the skillet. Drain the pasta and add to the skillet with the chives. Season with salt and pepper. Toss well over low heat for 1 minute, then serve.

1

1

3

GOES WELL WITH
Serve with lightly steamed sea bean, a type of seaweed, gently tossed with a little melted butter.

Spaghetti with Tuna Sauce

 SERVES 4   PREP TIME: 10 minutes   COOKING TIME: 15 minutes

nutritional information per serving	493 cal, 8g fat, 1g sat fat, 8g total sugars, 0.8g salt

This is a terrific standby dish for those times when you have run out of ideas or are simply feeling tired.

INGREDIENTS

12 ounces dried spaghetti

2 tablespoons olive oil

1 garlic clove, peeled and kept whole

1 onion, chopped

4 tomatoes, chopped

3 (5-ounce) cans chunk light tuna in spring water, drained and flaked

2 tablespoons capers, rinsed (optional)

2 tablespoons chopped fresh parsley, or 1 tablespoon chopped fresh basil, or a pinch of dried oregano

salt and pepper

1. Bring a large saucepan of lightly salted water to a boil. Add the pasta, bring back to a boil, and cook for 8–10 minutes, or according to the package directions, until tender but still firm to the bite.

2. Meanwhile, heat the oil in a separate saucepan and add the garlic. When it has begun to brown, remove and discard it. Add the onion and tomatoes to the pan and cook over low heat, stirring occasionally, for 5 minutes.

3. Drain the pasta and transfer to the pan with the vegetables. Add the tuna and capers, if using, and toss over the heat for a few minutes, until heated through. Remove from the heat, season with salt and pepper, stir in the herbs, and serve immediately.

1   2   3

SOMETHING
DIFFERENT
You can add extra
ingredients, such
as a few chopped
canned anchovies or
sliced, pitted olives,
depending on what
you have at hand.

Salad Niçoise

 SERVES 4–6   PREP TIME: 10 minutes   COOKING TIME: 20–25 minutes

nutritional information **per serving**   405 cal, 14g fat, 3g sat fat, 4g total sugars, 1.2g salt

It is a matter of debate in culinary circles whether this Mediterranean salad should contain tomatoes, green beans, or hard-boiled eggs, but most renditions contain all these ingredients.

INGREDIENTS

12 ounces dried conchiglie (pasta shells)

2 tuna steaks, about ¾ inch thick

olive oil, for brushing

2 cups trimmed green beans

store-bought garlic vinaigrette, to taste

2 hearts of lettuce, leaves separated

3 extra-large hard-boiled eggs, halved

2 juicy tomatoes, cut into wedges

1 (2-ounce) can anchovy fillets in oil, drained

½ cup pitted ripe black olives or Niçoise olives

salt and pepper

1. Bring a large saucepan of lightly salted water to a boil. Add the pasta, bring back to a boil, and cook for 8–10 minutes, or according to the package directions, until tender but still firm to the bite. Drain and refresh in cold water.

2. Heat a ridged, cast-iron grill pan over high heat. Brush the tuna steaks with oil on one side, place oiled-side down on the hot pan, and chargrill for 2 minutes.

3. Lightly brush the top side of the tuna steaks with a little more oil. Turn the tuna steaks over, then season with salt and pepper. Continue chargrilling for an additional 2 minutes for rare or up to 4 minutes for well done. Let cool.

4. Meanwhile, bring a large saucepan of lightly salted water to a boil. Add the beans and return to a boil, then boil for 3 minutes. Drain and immediately transfer to a large bowl. Pour the garlic vinaigrette over the beans and stir together. Stir in the drained pasta.

5. To serve, line a large serving plate with lettuce leaves. Lift the beans and pasta out of the bowl, leaving the excess dressing behind, and pile them in the center of the plate. Break the tuna into large flakes and arrange it over the beans. Arrange the hard-boiled eggs, tomatoes, anchovy fillets, and olives on the plate. Drizzle with more vinaigrette, if required, and serve immediately.

Scallop Soup with Pasta

 SERVES 6

PREP TIME:
15 minutes

COOKING TIME:
10–15 minutes

nutritional information per serving	444 cal, 15g fat, 8g sat fat, 5g total sugars, 1.6g salt

If you're planning a formal dinner party, this elegant soup makes an ideal appetizer.

INGREDIENTS

1 pound shucked scallops

1½ cups whole milk

6½ cups vegetable stock

1⅔ cups frozen green peas

6 ounces dried tagliolini

5 tablespoons butter

2 scallions, finely chopped

¾ cup dry white wine

3 slices of prosciutto, cut into thin strips

salt and pepper

chopped fresh flat-leaf parsley, to garnish

crusty baguette, to serve

1. Slice the scallops in half horizontally and season with salt and pepper.

2. Pour the milk and stock into a saucepan, add a pinch of salt, and bring to a boil. Add the peas and pasta, bring back to a boil, and cook for 8–10 minutes, or according to the package directions, until the pasta is tender but still firm to the bite.

3. Meanwhile, melt the butter in a skillet. Add the scallions and cook over low heat, stirring occasionally, for 3 minutes. Add the scallops and cook for 45 seconds on each side. Pour in the wine, add the prosciutto, and cook for 2–3 minutes.

4. Stir the scallop mixture into the soup, taste, and adjust the seasoning, if necessary, and garnish with the parsley. Serve immediately with the baguette.

1

2

3

GOES WELL WITH
Serve with
bruschetta—thick
slices of lightly
toasted rustic
bread or baguette,
rubbed with
garlic and
drizzled with
olive oil.

Mussel & Pasta Soup

 SERVES 4

PREP TIME:
15 minutes

COOKING TIME:
35 minutes

nutritional information per serving	996 cal, 75g fat, 41g sat fat, 4g total sugars, 1.3g salt

This rich and filling soup is full of flavor and would make a great weekend lunch with some crusty bread.

INGREDIENTS

1½ pounds mussels, scrubbed and debearded

2 tablespoons olive oil

1 stick butter

2 ounces bacon, chopped

1 onion, chopped

2 garlic cloves, finely chopped

⅓ cup all-purpose flour

3 Yukon gold or white round potatoes, thinly sliced

4 ounces dried farfalle

1¼ cups heavy cream

1 tablespoon lemon juice

2 egg yolks

salt and pepper

2 tablespoons finely chopped fresh parsley, to garnish

1. Discard any mussels with broken shells or any that refuse to close when tapped. Bring a large, heavy saucepan of water to a boil. Add the mussels and oil and season with pepper. Cover tightly and cook over high heat for 5 minutes, or until the mussels have opened. Remove the mussels with a slotted spoon, discarding any that remain closed. Strain the cooking liquid through a cheesecloth-lined strainer and reserve 5 cups.

2. Melt the butter in a saucepan. Add the bacon, onion, and garlic and cook over low heat, stirring occasionally, for 5 minutes. Stir in the flour and cook, stirring, for 1 minute. Gradually stir in all but 2 tablespoons of the reserved cooking liquid and bring to a boil, stirring continuously. Add the potato slices and simmer for 5 minutes. Add the pasta and simmer for an additional 10 minutes.

3. Stir in the cream and lemon juice and season with salt and pepper. Add the mussels. Mix together the egg yolks and the remaining mussel cooking liquid, then stir the mixture into the soup and cook for 4 minutes, until thickened.

4. Ladle the soup into warm bowls, garnish with chopped parsley, and serve immediately.

Basic Tomato Sauce *98*

Classic Pesto *100*

Roasted Garlic & Herb Sauce *102*

Simple Butter Sauce *104*

Lemon & Tarragon Sauce *106*

Creole Sauce *108*

Four Cheese Sauce *110*

Red Wine Sauce *112*

Sun-Dried Tomato Sauce *114*

Mushroom Sauce *116*

Arrabiata Sauce *118*

Chipotle Sauce *120*

Seafood Sauce *122*

White Wine Sauce *124*

Sauces

Basic Tomato Sauce

 SERVES 4   PREP TIME: 15 minutes   COOKING TIME: 25–30 minutes

nutritional information per serving	124 cal, 11g fat, 4g sat fat, 5g total sugars, 0.2g salt

There is no question that this is Italy's most favorite sauce for serving with pasta as well as other ingredients.

INGREDIENTS

2 tablespoons butter

2 tablespoons olive oil

1 onion, finely chopped

1 garlic clove, finely chopped

1 celery stalk, finely chopped

1 (14½-ounce) can diced tomatoes or 8 plum tomatoes, peeled, cored, and chopped

2 tablespoons tomato paste

brown sugar, to taste

1 tablespoon chopped fresh herbs and/or 1–2 teaspoons dried herbs and/ or 1–2 bay leaves

½ cup water

salt and pepper

1. Melt the butter with the oil in a saucepan. Add the onion, garlic, and celery and cook over low heat, stirring occasionally, for 5 minutes, until softened.

2. Stir in the tomatoes, tomato paste, sugar to taste, the herbs, and water, and season with salt and pepper.

3. Increase the heat to medium and bring to a boil, then reduce the heat and simmer, stirring occasionally, for 15–20 minutes, until thickened. Use as required.

GOES WELL WITH
This all-purpose sauce may be served with almost any kind of pasta, especially ridged and curly types, and is also delicious baked with ravioli.

Classic Pesto

nutritional information per serving	144 cal, 13.5g fat, 3.5g sat fat, 0.3g total sugars, 0.2g salt

Pesto is delicious stirred into pasta, soups, and salad dressings. It is available in most supermarkets, but making your own gives a concentrated, fresh flavor.

INGREDIENTS

40 fresh basil leaves
3 garlic cloves, crushed
3 tablespoons pine nuts
½ cup finely grated Parmesan cheese
2–3 tablespoons extra virgin olive oil
salt and pepper

1. Rinse the basil leaves and pat them dry with paper towels. Put the basil leaves, garlic, pine nuts, and cheese into a food processor or blender and blend for 30 seconds or until smooth. Alternatively, pound all of the ingredients in a mortar with a pestle.

2. If you are using a food processor, keep the motor running and slowly add the olive oil. Alternatively, add the oil drop by drop while stirring briskly. Season with salt and pepper. Use as required.

COOK'S NOTE
You can make
this pesto a
day ahead and
keep it in the
refrigerator until
you are ready to
cook the pasta.

Roasted Garlic & Herb Sauce

 SERVES 4 — PREP TIME: 10 minutes — COOKING TIME: 35–40 minutes

nutritional information
per serving — 72 cal, 5g fat, 2g sat fat, 1g total sugars, trace salt

Roasting garlic gives it a wonderfully mild flavor and a deliciously creamy texture.

INGREDIENTS

1 garlic bulb

1 tablespoon olive oil

2 handfuls of mixed herbs, such as flat-leaf parsley, basil, thyme, and sage, coarse stems removed

¼ cup sour cream

salt and pepper

1. Preheat the oven to 400°F. Peel the outer papery layers from the garlic bulb but leave the individual cloves intact. Using a sharp knife, cut a ¼–½-inch slice off the top of the garlic to expose the cloves.

2. Put the bulb into a small ovenproof container, such as a ramekin (individual ceramic dish), and drizzle with the oil. Cover with aluminum foil and roast in the preheated oven for 35–40 minutes, until the cloves feel soft.

3. Remove from the oven and let stand until cool enough to handle, then squeeze out the pulp from each clove into a food processor or blender. Add the herbs and sour cream and process until combined, then reheat the sauce gently over low heat without boiling, if required. Season with salt and pepper and use as required.

1   2   3

COOK'S NOTE
You can buy a
special garlic roaster—
a small terra-cotta
tray with a bell-shape
cover. You could also
just wrap the oil-
drizzled garlic bulb
in aluminum foil.

Simple Butter Sauce

SERVES 4

PREP TIME:
10 minutes

COOKING TIME:
15 minutes

nutritional information per serving	562 cal, 26g fat, 15g sat fat, 2g total sugars, 0.5g salt

Delicious and made in minutes, this is a great way to serve any long pasta, such as linguine, for a midweek family meal.

INGREDIENTS

1 pound dried long pasta
1 stick butter
8 sage leaves, finely chopped
8 basil leaves, finely chopped
½ bunch of fresh flat-leaf parsley, finely chopped
6 fresh thyme sprigs, finely chopped
1 small bunch of chives, snipped
salt and pepper
freshly grated Parmesan cheese, to serve

1. Bring a large saucepan of lightly salted water to a boil. Add the pasta, bring back to a boil, and cook for 8–10 minutes, or according to the package directions, until tender but still firm to the bite.

2. Just before the pasta is ready, melt the butter in a saucepan over low heat. Drain the pasta and pour the melted butter into the pan with the pasta. Add all the herbs, season with salt and pepper, and toss until the pasta strands are coated and glistening.

3. Divide among warm plates and serve immediately, with the Parmesan cheese served separately.

2

2

2

SOMETHING
DIFFERENT
Vary the herbs to suit
your personal taste,
but be careful with
very pungent ones,
such as tarragon and
marjoram.

Lemon & Tarragon Sauce

 SERVES 4

PREP TIME:
5 minutes

COOKING TIME:
No cooking

nutritional information per serving	200 cal, 12g fat, 2g sat fat, 0.5g total sugars, trace salt

The sharpness of lemon and the hint of anise in tarragon make this a really refreshing combination.

INGREDIENTS

1 small bunch of tarragon
juice of ½ lemon
grated rind of 1 lemon
¼ cup olive oil
2 garlic cloves, coarsely chopped
4 fresh parsley sprigs
1 bunch of chives
salt

1. Pick off the leaves from the tarragon, put them into a food processor or blender with the lemon juice, lemon rind, oil, garlic, parsley, chives, and a generous pinch of salt, and process until thoroughly combined. Use as required.

SOMETHING DIFFERENT

For a sweeter flavor, substitute 2 tablespoons of orange juice and the grated rind of ½ an orange for the lemon juice and rind.

Creole Sauce

 SERVES 4   PREP TIME: 15 minutes   COOKING TIME: 35–40 minutes

nutritional information per serving	127 cal, 6.5g fat, 1g sat fat, 10g total sugars, 0.2g salt

Enjoy a taste of the Deep South with this vibrant, spicy sauce, the chopped okra lending it both characteristic flavor and thickness.

INGREDIENTS

2 tablespoons sunflower oil

1 red bell pepper, seeded and thinly sliced

1 green bell pepper, seeded and thinly sliced

1 onion, thinly sliced

2–3 garlic cloves, crushed

1 fresh red chile, seeded and chopped

1 teaspoon ground coriander

1 teaspoon ground cumin

4 ripe tomatoes, peeled and chopped

1¼ cups vegetable stock

10 okra pods, trimmed and chopped

1 tablespoon chopped fresh cilantro

salt and pepper

1. Heat the oil in a heavy saucepan, add the red and green bell peppers, onion, garlic, and chile and sauté, stirring frequently, for 3 minutes. Add the ground coriander and cumin and sauté, stirring frequently, for an additional 3 minutes.

2. Stir in the tomatoes and stock and bring to a boil. Reduce the heat and simmer, stirring occasionally, for 15 minutes, or until the sauce has reduced slightly.

3. Add the okra to the pan with salt and pepper and simmer for an additional 10–15 minutes, or until the sauce has thickened. Stir in the fresh cilantro and use as required.

Four Cheese Sauce

 SERVES 4

PREP TIME:
10 minutes

COOKING TIME:
8–10 minutes

nutritional information per serving	879 cal, 44g fat, 27g sat fat, 2.5g total sugars, 2.5g salt

This sauce is actually made in the serving dish containing the drained pasta, and it must be one of the quickest sauces to prepare!

INGREDIENTS

1 pound dried tagliatelle

4 tablespoons butter

⅔ cup crumbled Gorgonzola cheese or other blue cheese

3 ounces fontina cheese, cut into narrow julienne strips

3 ounces Gruyère cheese, cut into julienne strips

3 ounces Parmesan cheese, cut into julienne strips

salt

1. Bring a large saucepan of lightly salted water to a boil. Add the pasta, bring back to a boil, and cook for 8–10 minutes, or according to the package directions, until tender but still firm to the bite.

2. Meanwhile, put the butter in a heatproof bowl set over a saucepan of barely simmering water. When it has melted, continue to heat it until hot but not boiling.

3. Drain the pasta and transfer to a warm serving bowl. Spread the cheeses on top and pour the hot butter over the cheeses and pasta. Toss lightly and serve immediately.

SOMETHING
DIFFERENT
You can substitute
strips of provolone for
the Gorgonzola for a
more subtle flavor.

Red Wine Sauce

 SERVES 4

PREP TIME:
10 minutes

COOKING TIME:
20 minutes

nutritional information per serving	240 cal, 20g fat, 10g sat fat, 2.5g total sugars, 0.6g salt

Mushrooms are more usually cooked with white wine, but the robust earthy flavor of wild mushrooms is perfectly complemented with red wine in this sauce.

INGREDIENTS

¾ stick butter

12 ounces mixed wild mushrooms, halved or quartered, if large

2 garlic cloves, finely chopped

1 tablespoon olive oil

¼ cup tomato paste

1 cup full-bodied red wine

½ cup pitted and halved ripe black olives

1 tablespoon chopped fresh parsley

salt and pepper

1. Melt 2 tablespoons of the butter in a skillet, add the mushrooms, sprinkle with a little salt, and cook over high heat, stirring occasionally, for 5 minutes.

2. Reduce the heat under the skillet to low, stir in the garlic and oil, and cook for 2 minutes, then stir in the tomato paste and cook for an additional 2 minutes.

3. Pour in the wine and cook for about 5 minutes, until the alcohol has evaporated. Meanwhile, dice the remaining butter. Add the butter to the skillet, one pat at a time, gently swirling the skillet until the butter has melted. Stir in the olives, season with salt and pepper, and remove the skillet from the heat. Sprinkle with parsley and use as required.

Sun-Dried Tomato Sauce

 SERVES 4   PREP TIME: 10 minutes   COOKING TIME: 15–20 minutes

nutritional information per serving	600 cal, 18g fat, 1.5g sat fat, 13g total sugars, 0.2g salt

Sun-dried tomatoes give this almost instant sauce an intense depth of sweet flavor.

INGREDIENTS

sauce

3 tablespoons olive oil

2 large onions, sliced

2 celery stalks, thinly sliced

2 garlic cloves, chopped

1 (14½-ounce) can diced tomatoes

1 cup drained and chopped
sun-dried tomatoes in oil

2 tablespoons tomato paste

1 tablespoon dark brown sugar

about ⅔ cup white
wine or water

salt and pepper

1. Heat the oil in a skillet. Add the onions and celery and cook until translucent. Add the garlic and cook for 1 minute. Stir in all the tomatoes, tomato paste, sugar, and wine and season with salt and pepper. Bring to a boil and simmer for 10 minutes. Use as required.

1   1   1

GOES WELL WITH

Use this flavorsome sauce in a meat or vegetable lasagne or serve with any pasta with a robust meaty filling.

Mushroom Sauce

 SERVES 4

PREP TIME:
10 minutes

COOKING TIME:
20 minutes

nutritional information
per serving

746 cal, 43g fat, 20g sat fat, 5g total sugars, 0.3g salt

This is a delicious pasta sauce, which uses sun-dried tomatoes and cremini mushrooms. It's made even more luxurious with the addition of heavy cream and port.

INGREDIENTS

4 tablespoons butter
1 tablespoon olive oil
6 shallots, sliced
1 pound cremini mushrooms, sliced
1 teaspoon all-purpose flour
⅔ cup heavy cream
2 tablespoons port
¾ cup drained and chopped sun-dried tomatoes in oil
pinch of freshly grated nutmeg
salt and pepper

1. Melt the butter with the oil in a large, heavy skillet. Add the shallots and cook over low heat, stirring occasionally, for 4–5 minutes, or until softened. Add the mushrooms and cook over low heat for an additional 2 minutes. Season with salt and pepper, sprinkle in the flour and cook, stirring, for 1 minute.

2. Remove the skillet from the heat and gradually stir in the cream and port. Return to the heat, add the sun-dried tomatoes and grated nutmeg, and cook over low heat, stirring occasionally, for 8 minutes. Use as required.

TO SERVE
Nutmeg is used widely in Italian cooking as it has a fragrant, sweet aroma. Use freshly grated nutmeg rather than ground, which rapidly deteriorates. Store it in an airtight container.

Arrabiata Sauce

 SERVES 4   PREP TIME: 15 minutes   COOKING TIME: 30 minutes

nutritional information per serving	518 cal, 16g fat, 2.5g sat fat, 6g total sugars, trace salt

Serve this tangy hot tomato sauce with pasta shapes, such as penne, or spaghetti. Unlike many other tomato sauce and pasta dishes, it is not traditionally served with grated Parmesan cheese.

INGREDIENTS

⅔ cup dry white wine

1 tablespoon tomato paste

2 fresh red chiles, seeded and chopped

2 garlic cloves, finely chopped

¼ cup chopped fresh flat-leaf parsley

salt and pepper

3 ounces pecorino cheese shavings

sugocasa

⅓ cup extra virgin olive oil

8 plum tomatoes, chopped

salt and pepper

1. To make the sugocasa, heat the oil in a frying pan over a high heat until almost smoking. Add the tomatoes and cook, stirring frequently, for 2–3 minutes.

2. Reduce the heat to low and cook gently for 20 minutes, or until very soft. Season with salt and pepper. Press through a nonmetallic strainer into a saucepan.

3. Add the wine, tomato paste, chiles, and garlic to the sugocasa, and bring to a boil. Reduce the heat and simmer gently. Check and adjust the seasoning, then stir in the parsley and the cheese. Use as required.

Chipotle Sauce

SERVES 4

PREP TIME:
15 minutes plus
soaking time

COOKING TIME:
15 minutes

nutritional information per serving	166 cal, 16g fat, 1g sat fat, 3g total sugars, trace salt

Smoking jalapeño chiles to make chipotles gives them a delicious depth of flavor but they do remain fiery.

INGREDIENTS

2 ancho chiles, seeded

1 red bell pepper

1–2 chipotle or jalapeño chilies, drained

⅓ cup pine nuts

juice of ½ lime

2 garlic cloves, coarsely chopped

1 tablespoon olive oil

salt

1. Preheat the broiler. Meanwhile put the ancho chiles into a bowl, pour in enough hot water to cover, and let soak for 30 minutes.

2. Put the red bell pepper on a baking sheet and place under the broiler, turning occasionally, for about 15 minutes, until charred and blistered. Remove with tongs, put into a plastic food bag, tie the top, and let cool.

3. Drain the ancho chiles, reserving 1 tablespoon of the soaking liquid. Peel, seed, and coarsely chop the red bell pepper.

4. Put the ancho chiles, reserved soaking liquid, red bell pepper, chipotle chiles, pine nuts, 1 tablespoon of the lime juice, and the garlic into a food processor or blender and process to a smooth paste. With the motor running at low speed, add the oil and process until thoroughly combined. If the sauce is too thick, add a little more lime juice and process briefly again. Season with salt and use as required.

1
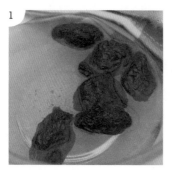

2

4

FREEZING TIP
Freeze the sauce
in an airtight
container for
1-2 weeks.

Seafood Sauce

 SERVES 4   PREP TIME: 10 minutes   COOKING TIME: 20–25 minutes

nutritional information per serving	232 cal, 10g fat, 2g sat fat, 0.2g total sugars, 0.9g salt

This is a great pasta sauce for informal entertaining because it is so quick and easy to make.

INGREDIENTS

1½ pounds fresh clams, or 1 (10-ounce) can clams, drained

2 tablespoons olive oil

2 garlic cloves, finely chopped

1 (14-ounce) package mixed prepared seafood, such as shrimp, squid, and mussels, defrosted if frozen

⅔ cup white wine

⅔ cup fish stock

2 tablespoons chopped fresh tarragon

salt and pepper

1. If using fresh clams, scrub them clean and discard any that are already open.

2. Heat the oil in a large skillet. Add the garlic and clams and cook for 2 minutes, shaking the skillet to make sure that all of the clams are coated in the oil. Add the remaining seafood to the skillet and cook for an additional 2 minutes.

3. Pour the wine and stock over the mixed seafood and garlic and bring to a boil. Cover the skillet, then lower the heat and simmer for 8–10 minutes, or until the shells open. Discard any clams that do not open.

4. Stir the tarragon into the sauce and season with salt and pepper. Use as required.

White Wine Sauce

 SERVES 4

PREP TIME:
10 minutes

COOKING TIME:
25–30 minutes

nutritional information
per serving | 844 cal, 77g fat, 48g sat fat, 4.5g total sugars, 1.2g salt

This rich, creamy sauce goes well with filled pasta such as ravioli—use a stock that matches the filling for extra flavor.

INGREDIENTS

1 Bermuda onion, chopped

5 cups dry white wine

10½ cups vegetable, chicken or fish stock

5 cups heavy cream

3 sticks butter

bunch of fresh flat-leaf parsley, finely chopped

salt and pepper

1. Put the onion in a large saucepan, pour in the wine, bring to a boil, and cook over high heat for 10 minutes, until the wine has almost completely evaporated.

2. Pour in the stock, return to a boil, and cook for 10-15 minutes, until it has reduced by two-thirds.

3. Stir in the cream and cook for 5 minutes, then stir in the butter, a little at a time. Add the parsley, season to taste with salt and pepper, and use as required.

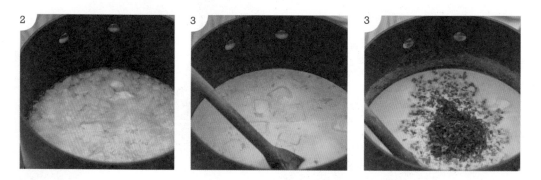

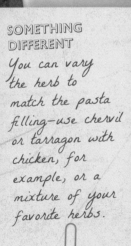

SOMETHING
DIFFERENT
You can vary
the herb to
match the pasta
filling—use chervil
or tarragon with
chicken, for
example, or a
mixture of your
favorite herbs.

Index

almonds
Mushroom Cannelloni 30
anchovies
Salad Niçoise 90
Spaghetti with Tuna & Parsley 84
Arrabiata Sauce 118
arugula
Pappardelle with Cherry Tomatoes,
Arugula & Mozzarella 34
Tagliatelle with Smoked Salmon &
Arugula 76
Ziti with Arugula 24
asparagus
Penne with Asparagus & Blue Cheese 16

bacon
Mussel & Pasta Soup 94
Pasta with Bacon & Tomatoes 62
Spaghetti with Bacon & Crispy Bread
Crumbs 54
Basic Tomato Sauce 98
basil
Classic Pesto 100
Pasta Salad with Melon & Shrimp 80
Sicilian Swordfish Pasta 72
Simple Butter Sauce 104
Tomato, Olive & Mozzarella Pasta
Salad 10
beans
Hearty Bean & Pasta Soup 32
beef
Hamburger Pasta 52
Lasagna al Forno 42
Spaghetti & Corned Beef 50
Spaghetti with Meat Sauce 38
bell peppers
Creole Sauce 108
Farfalle with Chicken & Broccoli 44
Pasta with Chicken & Bell Peppers 46
Pepperoni Pasta 48
Salmon Lasagna Rolls 82
Spicy Vegetable Lasagna 26
Tuna Noodle Casserole 68

bread
Spaghetti with Bacon & Crispy Bread
Crumbs 54
Tuna Noodle Casserole 68
Turkey Pasta Casserole 40
broccoli
Chile Broccoli Pasta 20
Farfalle with Chicken & Broccoli 44
butter
Four Cheese Sauce 110
Mushroom Sauce 116
Simple Butter Sauce 104
White Wine Sauce 124

cannelloni
Mushroom Cannelloni 30
Spinach & Ricotta Cannelloni 12
capers
Sicilian Swordfish Pasta 72
Spaghetti with Tuna Sauce 88
cheese
Arrabiata Sauce 118
Classic Pesto 100
Four Cheese Sauce 110
Hamburger Pasta 52
Hearty Bean & Pasta Soup 32
Lasagna al Forno 42
Macaroni & Double Cheese 8
Mushroom Cannelloni 30
Pappardelle with Cherry Tomatoes,
Arugula & Mozzarella 34
Pasta with Bacon & Tomatoes 62
Penne with Asparagus & Blue Cheese 16
Salmon Lasagna Rolls 82
Simple Butter Sauce 104
Spaghetti Carbonara 60
Spinach & Ricotta Cannelloni 12
Tomato, Olive & Mozzarella Pasta Salad
Salad 10
Tuna Noodle Casserole 68
Turkey Pasta Casserole 40
Ziti with Arugula 24

chicken
Chicken with Creamy Penne 64
Farfalle with Chicken & Broccoli 44
Pasta with Chicken & Bell Peppers 46
chiles
Arrabiata Sauce 118
Chile Broccoli Pasta 20
Chipotle Sauce 120
Creole Sauce 108
Hamburger Pasta 52
Linguine with Clams in Tomato Sauce 74
Pasta with Harissa Turkey Meatballs 56
Ziti with Arugula 24
Chipotle Sauce 120
chives
Lemon & Tarragon Sauce 106
Linguine with Shrimp & Scallops 86
Simple Butter Sauce 104
cilantro
Creole Sauce 108
Pasta with Leek & Butternut Squash 28
clams
Linguine with Clams in Tomato Sauce 74
Seafood Sauce 122
Classic Pesto 100
cod
Spaghetti & Cod 70
conchiglie
Hamburger Pasta 52
Salad Niçoise 90
Tomato, Olive & Mozzarella Pasta
Salad 10
cream
Chicken with Creamy Penne 64
Mushroom Sauce 116
Mussel & Pasta Soup 94
Roasted Garlic & Herb Sauce 102
Spaghetti Carbonara 60
White Wine Sauce 124
crème fraîche
Spaghetti with Tuna & Parsley 84
Creole Sauce 108

eggs
Lasagna al Forno 42
Mussel & Pasta Soup 94
Pasta with Harissa Turkey Meatballs 56
Salad Niçoise 90
Spaghetti Carbonara 60

farfalle
    Farfalle with Chicken & Broccoli 44
    Hearty Bean & Pasta Soup 32
    Mussel & Pasta Soup 94
    Pasta with Leek & Butternut Squash 28
Four Cheese Sauce 110
Fresh Tomato Soup with Pasta 14
fusilli
    Pasta Salad with Melon & Shrimp 80

garlic
    Classic Pesto 100
    Creole Sauce 108
    Lemon & Tarragon Sauce 106
    Penne Pasta with Sausage 58
    Red Wine Sauce 112
    Roasted Garlic & Herb Sauce 102
    Spaghetti & Corned Beef 50
    Spaghetti Olio E Aglio 22
    Sun-Dried Tomato Sauce 114

Hamburger Pasta 52
harissa
    Pasta with Harissa Turkey Meatballs 56
Hearty Bean & Pasta Soup 32
herbs
    Basic Tomato Sauce 98
    Roasted Garlic & Herb Sauce 102

lasagna
    Lasagna al Forno 42
    Salmon Lasagna Rolls 82
    Spicy Vegetable Lasagna 26
leeks
    Pasta with Leek & Butternut Squash 28
Lemon & Tarragon Sauce 106
lettuce
    Pasta Salad with Melon & Shrimp 80
lime
    Chipotle Sauce 120
linguine
    Linguine with Clams in Tomato Sauce 74
    Linguine with Shrimp & Scallops 86
    Sicilian Swordfish Pasta 72
long pasta
    Simple Butter Sauce 104

macaroni
    Chile Broccoli Pasta 20
    Macaroni & Double Cheese 8
    Turkey Pasta Casserole 40
marinade for chicken 46
meat sauce 38
melon
    Pasta Salad with Melon & Shrimp 80
mushroom soup
    Tuna Noodle Casserole 68
mushrooms
    Mushroom Cannelloni 30
    Mushroom Sauce 116
    Red Wine Sauce 112
    Salmon Lasagna Rolls 82
    Spaghetti with Meat Sauce 38
    Spicy Vegetable Lasagna 26
mussels
    Mussel & Pasta Soup 94
    Seafood Sauce 122

okra
    Creole Sauce 108
olive oil
    Arrabiata Sauce 118
    Classic Pesto 100
    Lemon & Tarragon Sauce 106
    Spaghetti Olio E Aglio 22
olives
    Mushroom Cannelloni 30
    Red Wine Sauce 112
    Salad Niçoise 90
    Sicilian Swordfish Pasta 72
    Tomato, Olive & Mozzarella Pasta
      Salad 10
onions
    Basic Tomato Sauce 98
    Creole Sauce 108
    Mussel & Pasta Soup 94
    Penne Pasta with Sausage 58
    Penne with Squid & Tomatoes 78
    Pepperoni Pasta 48
    Salmon Lasagna Rolls 82
    Spaghetti & Corned Beef 50
    Spaghetti with Tuna Sauce 88
    Sun-Dried Tomato Sauce 114
    White Wine Sauce 124

orecchiette
    Pasta with Bacon & Tomatoes 62
oregano
    Pasta with Bacon & Tomatoes 62
    Penne Pasta with Sausage 58
pancetta
    Lasagna al Forno 42
    Spaghetti Carbonara 60
pappardelle
    Pappardelle with Cherry Tomatoes,
      Arugula & Mozzarella 34
parsley
    Arrabiata Sauce 118
    Lemon & Tarragon Sauce 106
    Linguine with Clams in Tomato Sauce 74
    Pasta Salad with Melon & Shrimp 80
    Scallop Soup with Pasta 92
    Simple Butter Sauce 104
    Spaghetti Olio E Aglio 22
    Spaghetti with Tuna & Parsley 84
    Spaghetti with Tuna Sauce 88
    White Wine Sauce 124
Pasta with Bacon & Tomatoes 62
peas
    Chicken with Creamy Penne 64
    Scallop Soup with Pasta 92
penne
    Chicken with Creamy Penne 64
    Chile Broccoli Pasta 20
    Penne Pasta with Sausage 58
    Penne with Asparagus & Blue Cheese 16
    Penne with Squid & Tomatoes 78
    Pepperoni Pasta 48
Pepperoni Pasta 48
pesto
    Classic Pesto 100
pine nuts
    Chipotle Sauce 120
    Classic Pesto 100
    Mushroom Cannelloni 30
    Spaghetti with Bacon & Crispy Bread
      Crumbs 54
    Tomato, Olive & Mozzarella Pasta
      Salad 10
potatoes
    Mussel & Pasta Soup 94

prosciutto
　Scallop Soup with Pasta 92
Pumpkin Ravioli 18

ravioli
　Pumpkin Ravioli 18
Red Wine Sauce 112
Roasted Garlic & Herb Sauce 102

sage
　Simple Butter Sauce 104
Salad Niçoise 90
salmon
　Salmon Lasagna Rolls 82
　Tagliatelle with Smoked Salmon &
　　Arugula 76
sausages
　Lasagna al Forno 42
　Penne Pasta with Sausage 58
　Pepperoni Pasta 48
scallions
　Scallop Soup with Pasta 92
scallops
　Linguine with Shrimp & Scallops 86
　Scallop Soup with Pasta 92
Seafood Sauce 122
shrimp
　Linguine with Shrimp & Scallops 86
　Pasta Salad with Melon & Shrimp 80
　Seafood Sauce 122
Sicilian Swordfish Pasta 72
Simple Butter Sauce 104
soup
　Fresh Tomato Soup with Pasta 14
　Hearty Bean & Pasta Soup 32
　Mussel & Pasta Soup 94
　Scallop Soup with Pasta 92

spaghetti
　Pasta with Chicken & Bell Peppers 46
　Pasta with Harissa Turkey Meatballs 56
　Sicilian Swordfish Pasta 72
　Spaghetti & Cod 70
　Spaghetti & Corned Beef 50
　Spaghetti Carbonara 60
　Spaghetti Olio E Aglio 22

Spaghetti with Bacon & Crispy Bread
　Crumbs 54
Spaghetti with Meat Sauce 38
Spaghetti with Tuna & Parsley 84
Spaghetti with Tuna Sauce 88
Spicy Vegetable Lasagna 26
spinach
　Hearty Bean & Pasta Soup 32
　Spinach & Ricotta Cannelloni 12
squash
　Pasta with Leek & Butternut Squash 28
squid
　Penne with Squid & Tomatoes 78
　Seafood Sauce 122
sugocasa 118
Sun-Dried Tomato Sauce 114
swordfish
　Sicilian Swordfish Pasta 72

tagliatelle
　Four Cheese Sauce 110
　Pasta with Harissa Turkey Meatballs 56
　Sun-Dried Tomato Sauce 114
　Tagliatelle with Smoked Salmon &
　　Arugula 76
　Tuna Noodle Casserole 68
tagliolini
　Scallop Soup with Pasta 92
tarragon
　Lemon & Tarragon Sauce 106
　Seafood Sauce 122
thyme
　Simple Butter Sauce 104
tomatoes
　Arrabiata Sauce 118
　Basic Tomato Sauce 98
　Chile Broccoli Pasta 20
　Creole Sauce 108
　Fresh Tomato Soup with Pasta 14
　Hamburger Pasta 52
　Hearty Bean & Pasta Soup 32
　Linguine with Clams in Tomato Sauce 74
　Macaroni & Double Cheese 8
　Mushroom Sauce 116
　Pappardelle with Cherry Tomatoes,
　　Arugula & Mozzarella 34

Pasta with Bacon & Tomatoes 62
Pasta with Chicken & Bell Peppers 46
Pasta with Harissa Turkey Meatballs 56
Penne Pasta with Sausage 58
Penne with Squid & Tomatoes 78
Pepperoni Pasta 48
Spaghetti & Cod 70
Spaghetti & Corned Beef 50
Spaghetti with Meat Sauce 38
Spaghetti with Tuna Sauce 88
Sun-Dried Tomato Sauce 114
Tomato, Olive & Mozzarella Pasta
　Salad 10
tuna
　Salad Niçoise 90
　Spaghetti with Tuna & Parsley 84
　Spaghetti with Tuna Sauce 88
　Tuna Noodle Casserole 68
turkey
　Pasta with Harissa Turkey Meatballs 56
　Turkey Pasta Casserole 40

vegetables
　Hamburger Pasta 52
　Spicy Vegetable Lasagna 26
vermouth
　Linguine with Shrimp & Scallops 86

white sauce 28
White Wine Sauce 124
wine
　Arrabiata Sauce 118
　Chicken with Creamy Penne 64
　Linguine with Clams in Tomato Sauce 74
　Penne with Squid & Tomatoes 78
　Red Wine Sauce 112
　Scallop Soup with Pasta 92
　Seafood Sauce 122
　Sun-Dried Tomato Sauce 114
　White Wine Sauce 124

yogurt
　Pasta with Harissa Turkey Meatballs 56

Ziti with Arugula 24
zucchini
　Salmon Lasagna Rolls 82